VIEWS FROM THE DARK SIDE
OF AMERICAN HISTORY

CONFLICTING WORLDS

New Dimensions of the American Civil War

T. Michael Parrish, Series Editor

VIEWS FROM THE DARK SIDE
OF
AMERICAN HISTORY

Michael Fellman

Louisiana State University Press)|(*Baton Rouge*

Published by Louisiana State University Press
Copyright © 2011 by Louisiana State University Press
All rights reserved
Manufactured in the United States of America
LSU Press Paperback Original
First printing

Designer: Michelle A. Neustrom
Typefaces: Whitman, text; Tribute, display
Printer and binder: McNaughton & Gunn, Inc.

LIBRARY OF CONGRESS CATALOGING-IN-PUBLICATION DATA

Fellman, Michael.
Views from the dark side of American history / Michael Fellman.
    p. cm. — (Conflicting worlds : new dimensions of the American Civil War)
    ISBN 978-0-8071-3902-8 (pbk. : alk. paper) — ISBN 978-0-8071-3903-5 (pdf) — ISBN 978-0-8071-3904-2
(epub) — ISBN 978-0-8071-3905-9 (mobi) 1. Fellman, Michael. 2. Historians—United States—Biography.
3. Historiography—United States. 4. United States—Historiography. 5. United States—History—Study and
teaching (Higher) I. Title.
    E175.5.F38A3 2011
    907.2'02—dc22

                                                                                                    2011006961

Portions of chapter 1, "Madison Daze," were first published in *Labour/Le Travail* 29 (Spring 1992): 221–27.
Reprinted with permission of *Labour/Le Travail*.

Portions of chapter 3, "At the Nihilist Edge: Reflections on Guerrilla Warfare during the American Civil War,"
were first published in Förster, Stig and Jorg Nagler, eds. *On the Road to Total War: The American Civil War and
the German Wars of Unification, 1861–1871*. Cambridge: Cambridge University Press, 1997. Reprinted with the
permission of Cambridge University Press.

Portions of chapter 4, "Alligatormen and Cardsharpers: Deadly Southwestern Humor," were first published
in *Huntington Library Quarterly* 49 (Autumn 1986): 307–23. Reprinted with permission of the Huntington
Library Press.

Portions of chapter 5, "Robert E. Lee: Man and Myth," were first published in Wallenstein, Peter, and Bertram
Wyatt-Brown, eds. *Virginia's Civil War*. Charlottesville: University of Virginia, 2004. Reprinted with permission
of University of Virginia Press.

For Mike Zuckerman, Chris Phelps, and
for the memory of Bob Wiebe

CONTENTS

VIEWS FROM THE DARK SIDE
OF AMERICAN HISTORY

Introduction

BLAME MIKE PARRISH. I'll get around to explaining that.

Like so many things in life, the idea for this book grew not from a plan but from a random discovery connected to a chance encounter. Several years ago I was cleaning out my history department office at Simon Fraser University as I prepared to move to another campus of the same institution to take up an appointment as director of the Graduate Liberal Studies Program. In two long days I filled eleven huge recycling boxes. Course outlines from 1973, mingled with copies of endless correspondence concerning a book I co-edited thirty years ago, were buried among innumerable departmental meeting minutes along with directives from layers and generations of administrators, academic trivia that accumulated willy-nilly. Amid the mountain of junk were a few relative gems—copies of sometimes less-than-kind book reviews I had written decades earlier, about which I could recall nothing, offprints of articles from the day in which one still mailed those wee pamphlets to friends and colleagues, and a conference paper on the subject of Jewish American historians writing about the African American slave personality, which you will find printed as the second chapter of this book.

A couple of weeks after this experience in personal-clearance archeology, I attended the annual meeting of the Southern Historical Association, although in what city I cannot recall. Wandering the "book floor," where publishers set up tables to hawk monographs and textbooks, I happened on the Louisiana State University Press booth, where my old friend Mike Parrish was holding court. Formerly an archivist at the Lyndon B. Johnson Presidential Library, Mike is now a professor of history at Baylor University and editor of an important series in Civil War history with Louisiana State University Press. I reckoned Mike might be amused by the story about the rediscovery of that paper as further evidence for the "absent-minded professor" psychological theory. He listened and asked some typically incisive questions, and then suggested—quite to my surprise—that I send it along to him if I had a chance. As I knew him to be a discerning reader whose interests and values intersected with mine, I photocopied this typewritten paper from the precomputer dark ages and mailed it off to him in a large envelop affixed with stamps. He wrote me back, suggesting that I might want to put together a collection of some of my essays, explained and tied together with stories such as those I had told him about this forgotten and unpublished piece. Being busy with a book-length manuscript, I sort of filed the idea. But at the next conference, Mike brought up the notion again, suggesting students and history readers in general might be interested in the human-level ways in which historical work is generated and contextualized. And then he said, with a devilish twinkle in his eye, that seeing as how I was senior now and already had paid my dues with lots of heavy-duty, archive-driven books replete with fat footnotes, perhaps it was now time for me to experiment in a freer form of writing—"Indulge yourself," he said.

That temptation closed the deal for me. And that is why I say that for the existence of this book, you should blame Mike Parrish.

Views from the Dark Side of History is both methodological and autobiographical in nature. Written over the past thirty years and incorporating a half-dozen essays—two of them previously unpublished and the others not widely available—this book seeks to elucidate some of the major personal and scholarly concerns of my career and my approach to history as art and experience, as well as research, applied theory, and analysis. The vicissitudes of the life that produced my works are of no particular importance in and of themselves (except to me), but they can be plumbed to illuminate broader meanings. My generation has lived through interesting times, often in conflictive ways, and my writing has amounted to an independent take on shared experiences. Most often I have explored the dark side of history—issues of domination, exploitation, political violence, racism, and the ordeals of war.

This book moves through my historical practice and life experiences more or less chronologically. In each chapter, I begin with a prologue for the piece, reprint the essay for readers to take in for themselves, and then offer a discussion about the work. I explore not only the intellectual and political contexts of the pieces, but also the personal elements involved in their creation—the people with whom I was arguing and agreeing, the settings in which the papers were given and published, and the subjective as well as the historical issues that I was trying to work through when I was writing. This approach is at the same time personal and political, as there has always been political purpose to what I write, political in the broadest senses of the word. My work has always emerged from my most compelling social and individual concerns. Much of the methodology is interdisciplinary, with special emphasis on social psychology, cultural anthropology, and to a lesser extent, comparative history.

Sometimes broad generalizations can be explored through considering the concrete, the idiosyncratic. Through analysis of a few focused essays I intend to contribute my two-cents worth to the discussion of how one comes to write history, why it is such an independent and personal as well as social act, and why it matters. I highlight the cultural and personal distances between when the essays were written and the present time. Recollection is altered by subsequent change; the passions of earlier times look different in the light of always-unexpected events that later rushed down the road.

As befits our narcissistic age, memoirs have become a primary literary form. Some are confessions, others packages of resentments, self-justifications, or self-celebrations. The genre is immodest even when the tone tends to self-deprecation; after all, these are books about the self, or at least that abstracted, rearranged, and cleaned-up version of the self—the persona—that one *wishes* were the "real story." The claim to authenticity of memoirs is based on the assertion that authors are writing about what they really know well, but they are bound to be just literary reconstructions parading a story line through an unevenly recalled welter of often-distorted and unreliable memories.

Historians' memoirs tend to discuss great teachers and important books, and to omit much about life experiences except for graduate school and a few notes about the students historians have taught in turn. Most historians—unlike movie stars and in common with other academics—

are reticent to engage overtly with the subjective elements of their work, connections many often deny with considerable heat. Some of this tendency owes to appropriate personal modesty. Some stems from the fact that most professors lead safe and uneventful lives, bound up in insulating institutions—especially tenure—that muffle the more dramatic aspects of life. But perhaps the greatest source of the impersonal nature of this subset of memoirs is what Peter Novick has termed their authors' subscription to the "myth of objectivity." Most historians are trained to avoid focus on the subjectivity of their scholarship because to concede that their work is significantly influenced by the personal would, in their professional eyes, open their publications to dismissal by their colleagues as nonobjective, unscientific. God forbid that there be no absolute line between fiction and nonfiction.

However, it did not take the postmodern linguistic turn to make it clear that history writing, like all writing, *is* personal, is an author's "construction," whatever else it might be. As I have told generations of students, subjects write history, objects don't: when they sit down to write they and only they are responsible for interpreting the evidence. The facts do not speak, nor do they choose and arrange themselves. To paraphrase what Carl Becker wrote nearly a century ago, each student must be his or her own historian.

This does not imply, however, that anything goes. One still must seek out archival and other sources, quote from them as accurately and contextually as possible, discern the central points of previous historiography, and exercise fairness and balance in selection and argument. You cannot just make it up or take it from others. It is your writing and you are responsible for being true to the collective ethics of discovery, choice, and interpretation. Central to this ethos is that you also must be as conscious as possible of your own role, your own imagination and values in the writing you do. In fact, appeal to a nonexistent code of impersonal objectivity prevents you from acknowledging the inescapable subjectivity central to writing history.

In this book I will use parts of my life as a historian and writer by dealing with myself as a "cultural artifact." For the purposes of this book, the innermost experiences I include are those I consider significant not just for me in a personal sense but because they also contain broader social implications. In much of my writing I have worked through some of my reactions—slowed, condensed, altered, arranged, and transformed into analytic narratives—that I have had to my life and times. Particularly, with the clarity of retrospection (although I may have barely been aware of some of these connections when I was writing), my history work reveals individual reactions to the American past refracted and redefined through the lenses created by the events through which I and many others viewed life.

This is not to say that history writing is bound to be essentially presentist, i.e., only interested in the here and now at the time of composition. It is to say that contemporary responses to cultural and personal events cause one to explore issues in historical contexts colored by current concerns. Yet at the same time one can respond to the very *pastness* of the past, that which is different rather than similar. Thus, for example, in my most recent book, *In the Name of God and Country: Reconsidering Terrorism in American History,* I discuss the now-archaic modes of expression contained in the mentality and religious values of John Brown at the same time that I try to understand him as a terrorist whose thought structures and violent practices are akin to those hyper-zealous religious terrorists haunting us now, particularly since 9/11. Moreover, I discuss Brown in the context of the kangaroo trial and quick execution that followed his capture not just to explain how the Virginia authorities reacted back in 1859, but also to begin to understand the counter-terrorist responses of the American state to terrorism in our own times. Of course ideologies and ideas change over time; but at the same time, all are concerned with certain primary human and social issues, then as now. The American past is not a foreign country; it has formed the templates by which we still think, act, and react.

At the micro-level of the individual historian, awareness of one's own inevitable biases and subjectivity can illuminate one's work through validating rather than suspecting imagination. When reacting to seminal events and subjecting them to rigorous analysis, we can begin to create tools to use in historical work. But this capacity for exploration will not grow unless we can free ourselves from the notion that we ought to "fit" within cultural frameworks, such as those produced by the rigorous hazing of graduate work, and to deny our individual experiences—rough and tumble as they may be—for our membership in a club of historians, in a university, or in a society that, despite abstract protestations of freedom of speech, sponsors conventional thinking and penalizes individuality of expression. In this sense, truly engaged history writing is anarchic or at least irreverent. It challenges authority; it is the assertion of freedom of thought against the constraints of received wisdom; it is the individual declaration that one need not be captured and neutralized by the powerful fear of being isolated and derided, that one can find one's own voice.

To move from the general to the specific, the values in which I was raised, and the unexpected voyages I have made, were common for many of those who were born around 1943 in places like Madison, Wisconsin. My experience of shared events was my own, and how I brought this sensibility to history writing was in a sense unique, but it led to my writing about shared experiences—a paradox of individuality and commonality that I cannot really sort out.

During the 1950s and1960s, my high school, Madison West, was filled with academic brats, the children of scholars working at the relatively progressive University of Wisconsin. There was less anti-intellectual sentiment in my school, especially among my large group of friends, than was the case in most places in the United States at the time, pockets in New York and San Francisco notwithstanding. Yet Wisconsin, the home of La Follette progressivism, was also the state of Senator Joe McCarthy, the violently destructive redbaiter who cast a pall over the whole American society of the day. I try to correct for nostalgia and deromanticize my version of the Wisconsin of my youth, even if it was the place where I was nurtured in an easy and happy immediate social environment. McCarthy was impossible to overlook, even for an eleven-year-old, and I began to learn from him about the dark side of politics at the same time that I absorbed the hopes of the progressive forces with whom my father and many of his friends were joined. (The Army-McCarthy Hearings were my first television experience, and I remember that the glowering, nasty senator seemed part buffoon, part Really, Really Bad Guy.) At best, politics was an intense struggle against the forces of reaction that most often seemed nearly overwhelmingly powerful (and still do). A dawning awareness of the Holocaust heightened this early response to the ruthless nastiness of American political reaction.

I moved into young adulthood and graduate school during the ever-turbulent 1960s, and as was true of nearly everyone I knew, I was deeply moved and disturbed, sometimes to action, by the civil rights movement and the war in Vietnam. Not only did these times lead many of us to active political engagement, they influenced the choice of historical subjects we made and colored the ways in which we made our analyses. Although it is hard to recapture the political and personal earnestness in our current, endlessly ironic times, back then we were impelled by what now seem rather naive moral imperatives. There was to be no boundary between our civil and scholarly lives—all parts of our experiences seemed relevant to all other parts, particularly when we were full of the energy and arrogance of those in their twenties, in a generation engaged in unusually open conflict with our elders and the institutions they had created. We believed our history writing should connect to our activism, as if what we said and wrote and how we demonstrated in the streets all might combine to contribute to progressive change in which we truly believed.

And yet there was something in me, some innate skepticism, which led me to question the excesses of my generation, including my own angriest and most adventurist impulses. I was always wary of the tendency to authoritarianism, even of those on "my side." This detachment grew when the antiwar movement split, some of it moving toward embracing violence in 1967. The following year, when I wrote my thesis on utopian communitariansim—very much a New Left topic about the anarchic end of the liberal spectrum—I was beginning to change my mind about the dogmatism and harshly self-righteous combativeness of many of those with whom I was in basic agreement. Certainly the government and other major institutions the New Left was struggling against were far more efficient and thorough employers of political violence, and would remain my major concern as they maintained the monopoly of power. Just that the good-versus-evil narrative was far too simple, self-serving, and blinding to be accepted as the way to do good history, or for that matter, effective politics. This step back, which was reflected in the way I approached the communitarians, did not lead to social disengagement, but it did lead to separation from groups of historians who were there on the barricades where I had joined them in demonstrations but not in dogma or, finally, partisanship. These are all themes I sort through in the chapters that follow, when my cussed independent streak kept me from complete psychological, ideological, or physical immersion in the politics of the day.

And then in 1969, Ph.D. in hand, I moved to Vancouver, British Columbia. This move would make an enormous impact on me as a person and an American historian, giving me an unusual and constructive vantage point on my life and work.

But it was an accident, the opposite of a plan. The job market was very tight, and I didn't have a firm offer from an American university. Ohio State University was making noises of a sort but nothing concrete. In any event, a couple of weeks before the March convention of the Organization of American Historians, Don S. Kirschner, a professor of American history at the almost brand-new Simon Fraser University who had earned his Ph.D. at Iowa, wrote to his Iowa grad school chum George Daniels, who was my advisor, asking if he had anyone suitable for a job in the "Middle Period" of American history. George suggested me. In New York, I had a drink with Don and then a meeting with two or three more SFU historians at the decrepit Statler Hilton hotel, and two weeks later, without a campus visit, I was offered a tenure-track job. As the University of British Columbia had a two-year appointment for my wife, and with Vancouver sounding like a hippie idyll and Canada well out of the terrible war, off we went, young and eager for change.

Some of my experiences at Simon Fraser proved to be quite difficult (as I will discuss later), but much of life in Vancouver was splendid, and I could get on with teaching and writing, not unallied to dance parties and camping trips. My teaching took on a political coloration immediately, as all my courses were fully subscribed, almost half by some of the thousands of American deserters and draft dodgers and their girlfriends then pouring into Canada. I shared the cultural styles of nonauthoritarian instruction, African love beads, madras shirts, long hair, and mellow smokes with my students, many of whom were approximately my age. Somehow most of the people I knew assumed that I was a draft dodger, and although I honored those young men for their political decision, I could not claim that title. But the media wanted to talk with someone in a position of apparent authority who could represent the flood of visitors, about which most Canadians were quietly rather pleased— Americans fleeing their homeland and coming to Canada for political freedom was an interesting irony. I certainly identified with my students and was against the war, so I was engaged with the antiwar movement from across the 49th parallel.

Eventually the war ended, the generation gap dissipated, and my public role shifted more toward trying to explain American politics and history to Canadians without pandering to their tendency to national smugness. My standard joke was that I was equally alienated from two societies. This "man-without-a-country" stance fed my historical impulse to challenge all nationalist patriotisms—a good thing in a historian in my opinion, then and now.

But it has been more than forty years since I changed countries, and although I hold citizenship and pay taxes in both places, I would have to say that, ever since Ronald Reagan's presidency, I have felt more profoundly alienated from the land of my birth. This sentiment was only accentuated by the George W. Bush regime. In the nation of my accidental move, the current Tory rule smacks of Right-wing American Republicanism, but I am not convinced they have swept all before them. All immigrants experience a disjuncture between their natal land as it was when they left and the new place into which it has morphed over time. Although remaining in North America and frequently visiting the place of my birth, I feel a special form of alienation through this discontinuity of residence. I have remained just outside many of the cultural changes in the United States.

Yet I believe that this move across the border has given me an unusual and constructive long-term perspective on the alterations in American society that have occurred during those four decades. To me, the greatest change to affect the America of my birth has been the permanent militarization of its society, not only with nearly perpetual wars abroad but also with a corrosive impact on the homeland. Especially since 9/11 there has been an atmosphere—stirred up by the government—of interminable fear and loathing of presumably threatening aliens, coupled with the unconstitutional and draconian punishment of suspected terrorists, that has undercut the spirit of liberty and freedom for all that is the most trumpeted advertisement of the United States. Self-righteous dogma about the unique moral value of the City upon a Hill has served to disguise much evil done in the name of protecting the security of that vision, including torture and long-term imprisonment without a hearing and without charges.

While militarism and its effects, such as a fetishistic gun culture and the excessive use of incarceration for young men of nonwhite races, has colored the land of my birth, I believe that many Americans, including many American historians, have celebrated the country's history as exceptional, which means better than that of any other nation. This patriotic sensibility has strongly influenced mainstream American Civil War history, a subject I will discuss in subsequent chapters. This exaltation has rather immediate political implications of supporting militarism and war as presumably useful means by which to solve larger social issues.

My offshore perspective has been, I believe, a positive tool to help explore these darkest of qualities in the modern United States. Canada is considerably different in many ways, a place that has never entirely abandoned the ideal of a supportive community nor engaged in the building of a huge military to participate in endless wars with all the social ramifications militarism contains.

Of course many other American intellectuals have moved to Canada, but this book reflects on my experience of what to do with the paradox of double alienation, making it a tool of constructive engagement between two nations. As a committed skeptic and agnostic, I feel rather like a historian forever coming from abroad, never quite landing. Stemming from this deracinated perspective, I have always encouraged my students to find their own voices rather than imitate others. All students of history can sort through their life experiences, their own sets of tensions and contradictions, swim away from the coast of nationalism, and work from there.

I believe that our special role as historians is to challenge unthinking submission to power and domination. All of us are subject to great (if often unstated) ideological and political pressures to accept, rather than to combat, social discrimination along lines of race, class, gender, ethnicity, and nationality. There is a generally asserted and rather smug belief that American society has overcome such modes of prejudice, something it has done to a certain extent but not deep below the surface. The forces of discrimination regroup with considerable flexibility under new banners, and one must come to understand the continuing power of such attitudes. But one also can learn to resist even the subtlest forms of repression and oppression when thinking about and writing history. Done right, this is an individual, independent, and socially critical act. Sometimes hard and lonely, it is the very place where each historian can develop her or his unique perspective.

1

Madison Daze

REMEMBERING THAT I HAD been born and bred in Madison, Wisconsin, my former Simon Fraser University colleague Bryan Palmer, who had moved on to Queen's University (and subsequently would go to Trent University), asked me to review a collection of essays edited by Paul Buhle on Madison "in the day." I saw no good reason to keep my autobiography out of my review; particularly as this was a grouping of memoirs, my form could mirror (and to a certain extent satirize) that of the authors. As the essay indicates, although my father taught at the University of Wisconsin, and although I grew up I knowing several of the authors as well as many of the faculty members of the history department at Wisconsin—some of whom remained life-long friends—I never studied there. Therefore I was both insider and outsider when I reviewed this collection.

Much of the heat behind this essay—most of which, as I read it now, remained rather submerged—came from my own experiences as a radical graduate student during the Vietnam War. Both as a participant and a target, I experienced many of the divisions on the New Left, fundamental contradictions that contributed to its demise. Underlying this split was the deep and irresolvable disagreement about adopting political violence as a tactic, a subject about which I had deep convictions.

There is a second element, nostalgia—considered somewhat ironically —that also animated my writing. These were the good-old days when my generation was young, passionately committed, combative, and full

Portions of this chapter were first published in *Labour/Le Travail* 29 (Spring 1992): 221–27. "Madison Daze" was a review of Paul Buhle, ed. *History and the New Left: Madison, Wisconsin, 1950–1970.* Philadelphia: Temple University Press, 1990.

of music, Mary Jane, and sex. The temptation to indulge fond memories mixed with my innate and almost ruthless skepticism even concerning my own past. A somewhat jaded forty-nine-year-old wrote this reconsideration of that youthful time, when I had been a foot soldier among the New Left that was so amazingly alive, so frightened about the power of the American government, and yet so hopeful (well, somewhat hopeful in my case) about changing it root and branch.

American society had moved sharply to the right after the days these stories recalled, and so it was tempting to celebrate the grand battles in contrast to the gloom that had settled over the national landscape since. Therefore it seemed almost churlish, perhaps even defeatist, to consider the mistakes we ourselves had made—in a sense the fall from anticipated grace that we all experienced—particularly as larger and oppressive political forces accounted for most of the tragic loss this book and this review imply. My sympathies remained with the party of change, and they still do, but the realities of history overtook us all.

"*Madison Daze*"

As a Madison old boy I cannot approach this fascinating collection of essays as a pretended neutral. I was born in Madison, where my family moved permanently in 1947, when I was four, and I lived there until I went off on a European walkabout in 1961, a year prior to my entry into Oberlin College. My father, David Fellman, taught in the political science department of the University of Wisconsin for thirty years, creating the first course on civil liberties in an American university. He was a classic Progressive: as well as being an active scholar and teacher, he was deeply involved in campus and national political and cultural activities, most especially in Wisconsin liberal Democratic politics during its post-McCarthy resurgence. As well as writing Gaylord Nelson's most eloquent speeches during his successful 1958 gubernatorial campaign, which marked, even more than William Proxmire's election to the Senate a year earlier, the comeback of the Wisconsin Democratic Party, he also invented the Wisconsin Civil Rights Commission.

By 1965 I was a graduate student at Northwestern, and my father and

I had increasingly angry exchanges over the war in Vietnam, his support of which I believed to be a betrayal of the liberal values he had taught me and his students, and which he had helped enact in his very active public life. What I then believed to be my radicalism—and my thesis, written in 1968–1969, was on American communitarianism—I now see more as enraged liberalism, to which was added a youthful thirst for action, which, on the whole, I sublimated in libraries and archives.

This book makes quite clear that Madison, 1950–1970, was about radicalism in a liberal matrix, and about how the baby was thrown out with the bath water. Some of the thirty authors are more self-reflectively generous than others, some more self-serving and mean-spirited; some past events, usually the celebratory ones, are fully aired, while some of the painful ones are downplayed or nearly omitted. Taken as a whole this book is a very human and appealing rendering of an epoch of extraordinary *Sturm und Drang* in the Midwest.

The locale of the drama is very precisely Madison; culture and politics are intertwined with work and life in the history department. Although many of the authors writing here claim that they gained allegiance to European methods, theories, and culture while in Madison, and to a socialist perspective on national and international issues, it is the everyday, practical parochialism of their memories that is most vivid. Europe appears as books read and arguments asserted; even contemporary events at Berkeley, Michigan, and Columbia are mentioned one time each, although 1950s San Francisco bohemianism is an underlying presence in the book—viewed as Madison West. The over-riding retrospective concerns of these former students and their teachers are in fact local and concrete, protestations of cosmopolitanism notwithstanding. Indeed all three members of a long-ago love triangle write essays here, and you can piece together their tangled web if you have a mind to. The adage that history is just (higher) gossip is spelled out here, which is one of the reasons this is such an engaging collection.

At war during the 1950s with the conservative, Richard Hofstadter–led history department at Columbia, Madison's was the other great department in the United States, the Progressive one. From the time of Fighting Bob LaFollette and his powerful academic allies, including Frederick Jackson Turner, the father of modern American history, whose salad days were spent in Madison, the university, which proclaimed proudly that its boundaries were the boundaries of the state, was unusually open to educational experimentation and unconventional ideas. Not only was American labor studied seriously almost uniquely in Madison from the turn of the century, the university also created a School for Workers (unmentioned in these pages) which nurtured CIO as well as AFL organizers during summer seminars. In the 1930s, Alexander Meikeljohn, fired from Smith College, founded an Experimental College, quite a wild innovation for its time.

In the history department, by the early 1950s a remarkable group of Progressive historians had gathered. In American history, these included Merrill Jensen, Howard K. Beale, Fred Harvey Harrington, and, most notably, Merle Curti, who, among other activities, created American intellectual history, and who nurtured a wide range of young scholars, whose appreciation for him rings through many of these essays. Indeed some of these writers over-emphasize Curti's undoubted saintliness, underestimating the aggressive, left-wing political and cultural criticism which animates his best work. In this volume, James B. Gilbert best summarizes the "Wisconsin historical tradition, upheld and nourished by [this] remarkable group of scholars." These historians, Gilbert writes, "had been educated in a tradition that had deep roots in American Progressivism, and they exhibited its serious but attractive secular religiosity, its anti-establishment anger, its faith in the power and responsibility of government, and its firm belief that intellectuals ought to serve the state and the nation" (120).

Most of the authors writing here were attracted by the Wisconsin American historians, but they were also deeply influenced by Hans Gerth, a brilliant, complicated, and difficult sociologist, who was a survivor of the Frankfurt School of Weimar Germany, and by the writing of his great student, C. Wright Mills, by 1950 gone from Madison, but at the height of his tragically brief career; by George Mosse, an erudite, witty, and engaging European intellectual historian; by Harvey Goldberg, the very personification of French *gauchist* activism; and, absolutely central to this book, by William Appleman Williams, who studied in Madison after World War II and returned to teach in 1958, gathering around him many of the young scholars who originated the Madison New Left.

The students attracted to the Madison milieu of the 1950s were a mixture of midwestern WASPs and New York Jewish red diaper babies, Eugene Dennis, Jr., and Michael Meeropol, son of Julius and Ethel Rosenberg, included. Unlike the Ivy League, and prior to the creation of the State University of New York, Madison welcomed the children of the Old Left—indeed the last Labor Youth League of the Communist Party survived in Madison until the end of the 1950s. This group is well-represented in this collection. Most of them tell of discovering America in Madison, and of developing beyond sectarianism and dogmatism. Several stayed long enough to join the blossoming of the New Left.

Even during the trough of the Cold War, Communists joined Progressives in political and cultural activities that are joyfully recounted in these pages. Cultural activities included endless arguments at the Rathskeller in the Student Union, at the Green Lantern eating co-operative, at the 602 Club on University Avenue, listening to jazz, dressing in basic bohemian black. Political activities began with the Joe Must Go recall campaign, and at the end of the 1950s and the beginning of the 1960s, the creation of the "Anti-Military Ball," a satirical political counter-cultural response to the annual ROTC dance, the creation of a nonsectarian Socialist Club, sympathetic civil rights boycotts in Madison as well as in the South, and the Fair Play for Cuba Committee.

From within the history department, graduate students, mainly those studying with Williams, founded *Studies on the Left* in 1959. Although they were unevenly sophisticated in their abilities to execute essays, the ambitions of this young group were lofty and serious, as they attempted to wed socialist theory to Progressive empiricism and political engagement. *Studies on the Left* decamped for New York City in 1963, an event not fully analyzed here.

And then the war came. The *Studies*-Williams group, opposed to the war, consciously on the anti-Imperialist left, nevertheless remained, as James Gilbert writes, "cautious, intellectual, a bit cynical" about direct action (120). This was the cool jazz generation that would be displaced by a younger student left of rock 'n roll. Although discussion of this transition is rather elliptical in this volume, there are many clues here.

Elizabeth Ewan points out that to younger students like her, by 1964, Williams and the remaining *Studies* people seemed "rather remote" to younger radicals, while the spellbinder Harvey Goldberg "personified the spirit of activism" (150). Paul Buhle and others of the younger New Left founded *Radical America,* far more populist than had been *Studies,* and in campus politics tended more to spontaneity than to calm reflection. The climax of this second, direct action generation of the Madison New Left came in the sit-in against Dow Chemical on-campus interviews in October 1967, which ended in violence.

In comparison to the 1950s Old Left/midwest Progressive radicals, and to the *Studies* group, this generation is under-represented in these pages. From a glancing and ironic retrospective stance, Evan Stark, *the boy orator* of the 1966–67 sit-ins, describes how the media "reified [him] like a campus [beauty] queen." Looking back at his Madison persona, he now sees "one of a rare breed of post-adolescent gunfighters whose artillery consisted of rhetorical flamboyance mixed with Jewish humor and an almost inhuman capacity to attend meetings and walk the picket line after debating through the night" (174). Immediately after helping escalate the anti-Dow events into violence, Stark resigned from the university rather than awaiting the suspension that would have come, and disappeared from Madison. In general, this violent episode marked the final division of radicals from liberals and the passing of the central role of the Goldberg-activist New Left second generation. Sectarian fragmentation and nihilism ensued.

Post-1967 Madison appears only indirectly in these pages, as nearly all the authors were gone from Madison by this time, and as none joined the barbarian third generation New Left of 1967–71. As Buhle points out, by 1969 at the latest, the Madison left had disintegrated, and he, in common with every other contributor here, looks back in horror at the so-called Maoist "post–New Left gangs" whose form of radicalism ran to "hurling rocks through the State Street windows" of small businessmen (230). This cult of violent action led on directly to the horror of the 1971 bombing of the Army math research center on campus in which an innocent foreign graduate student was killed, and with him, the Madison left, except in pamphlet rhetoric.

Only William Appleman Williams (discussed below) in any way assumes responsibility for the final 1967–71 period of the Madison New Left. As for the others, did they or did they not help create, however unconsciously, the political culture which nourished the final nihilist phase? Did the first and second New Left generations provide the cultural matrix for the post-1967 crazies, in a sort of bizarre and speeded-up recapitulation of the manner in which, for two decades, Madison Progressives had nourished them? Lack of discussion of this issue is the most serious omission from this collection. Perhaps it was left out because of the pain such analysis would have recalled. Pushing into violence themselves in 1967, opening the door for subsequent mindless action factions, in retrospect, was pushing beyond reconstruction into destruction visited on radicals and liberals alike.

If not a guilty one, the underlying moral tone of the more human of these writers is one of profound regret about what was lost, and about all who were hurt in the process. In a brilliant essay, written in 1981, the late Eleanor Hakim, a 1950s existentialist-independent left Madisonian, recounts the tragedy of Hans Gerth, who ended his Madison days in the late 1960s, mocked and scorned by the younger New Left. For Hakim, this persecution personified the manner in which the New Left came to destroy an adult intellectual and cultural politique for the "easy allurements of political expediency" (258). Several other writers, including George Mosse and James Gilbert, also emphasize that an angry and destructive direct action moralism displaced historical analysis. Indeed analysis of any but the crudest anarchist sort virtually disappeared on the Madison New Left.

With considerable bitterness as well as regret, the late William Appleman Williams escaped Madison in 1968 for Oregon State University. In his retrospective view here, the 1947–50 period, when he had done his graduate work, had been a golden age when well-motivated veterans, like himself, as students, had studied in a wonderful arts faculty which was full of first-rate conservatives and feisty liberals as well as of radicals like himself and Hans Gerth. Of a religious and Annapolis background, Williams approached community and intellectual excellence as moral imperatives which demanded not only self-denial but the emotional and moral capacity to engage in dialogue with people of other minds, which called for, in Williams's phrase, the "necessity of walking the mile in the other person's shoes." This was precisely the place, he argues, where the Madison New Left failed, and this failure led on to the replacement of thoughtful criticism by increasingly "random and nonsocial violence," and of plausible political action by "moral determinism" and phony vanguardism. The New Left alienated their liberal protectors and allies, Williams argues, and he does not shift all the blame on to the post-1967 monsters, but accepts the possibility that the New Left had a continuous as well as a discontinuous moral history. "In later years," Williams writes of the lost liberal allies, "the Left has either forgotten them or castigated them as sunshine radicals. I want to salute them as people who demonstrated the capacity and courage for intellectual change and moral and emotional commitment. I think it was we who lost them instead of them betraying us" (270–71).

This profound and moving example of Williams's sense of moral and social responsibility surely is one of the reasons which led James Gilbert in his essay to deal with Williams as the last representative of the Madison Progressive school rather than as the first New Leftist. I believe that Williams would have rejected Gilbert's act of kindness, an act which makes a certain amount of historical sense, and that he would not have disowned his role in fostering the New Left even though the events that followed turned out to be repellant to him. His was not a convenient morality.

To return to the germination time of the Madison left, Richard Schickel, the brilliant *Time* magazine movie reviewer and writer of books of film criticism, who wrote energetic and clever radical editorials in the student newspaper in the early 1950s, recalls the impact of the University of Wisconsin on him. His experience, radicalism included, taught him to seek no "grand visions but simple . . . a sense of meaning, not The Meaning. . . . These are not, of course, values of the radical university. They are the values of the liberal one, the university that claimed my first, and now my last allegiance." Schickel reads the collected essays of the late Warren Sussman in this light, and George Mosse reads the post-Madison history writing produced by many of the contributors to these pages in a similar manner—intellectual productivity occurred on ground more modest than the dreamscapes of earlier days.

Until the late 1960s, this liberal university protected and nurtured generations of radical students. To take one salty example from the early 1950s of this liberal/radical paradigm, the Marxist George Rawick just hated what he found to be a reactionary hick Madison, Merle Curti excepted, when he arrived to do graduate work in 1951. He found most of the vaunted Progressive historians to be "weird old men," most particularly Howard K. Beale, who made sure that Rawick would receive no fellowship for a second year, declaring to Rawick that "no unwashed bohemian, no matter how brilliant," would get a Madison Ph.D. The next year, Merle Curti, who had been away from Madison while Beale was playing the right bastard, rescued Rawick from Western Reserve with a teaching Assistantship and a prestigious research fellowship. In 1957, when Rawick was defending his doctoral thesis and found himself being viciously red-baited by Paul Sharp, none other than Howard K. Beale rose to Rawick's defense, demanding that the red-baiting questions be withdrawn or else that he, Beale, would take the issue to Committee A, the Committee on Academic Freedom of the American Association of University Professors. Beale and Rawick won the argument, and this demonstrated to Rawick that after all, Beale's "civil libertarianism was real and strong" (55–57).

A nice story, one which the recently deceased Rawick doubtless dined out on for 40 years. But I suspect that the story was a good deal more ironic than Rawick's version. As Beale was declaiming during this defense, the office of the Chairman of Committee A of AAUP, David Fellman, was not more than a stone's throw away; Paul Sharp, who was quite junior in the history department, knew that Fellman would give him holy hell if he pursued his red-baiting into actions against Rawick, and Beale knew all this. Thus at very little risk to himself, Beale could play the courageous liberal in order to impress a radical graduate student he had previously attacked in a vicious and underhanded manner. In addition, Beale was hazing Sharp, and at the same time apologizing to his colleagues, Merle Curti in particular, for earlier having abused his own authority by savaging Rawick's career in the most illiberal manner, by judging him on the cut of his clothes rather than on the quality of his mind. Years earlier, in supporting Rawick, Curti had shamed Beale for his persecution of Rawick, a prime example of the sort of behavior which made the curmudgeon Beale so unpopular with his colleagues. At this examination, Beale was publicly reaffirming his shaky subscription to a liberal Madison consensus, one that was far sturdier, even in 1957, than Rawick realized. Rawick was far less embattled and heroic than he thought, and Madison politics were rather more complex than many radicals realized, even radicals who were defended for reasons other than the ones they fancied. All this is Madison past. The special liberal/radical stew is quite gone; Wisconsin is now just another good Big Ten university, not especially strong in the Arts; and no one would argue that the history department is the best in the United States, or can be characterized as special in any political or cultural sense, some fine professors and students notwithstanding. In the 1970s, the radical community did foster a teaching assistants trade union and the mayoralty of Paul Soglin, who proved rather astute and progressive. Recently, after several years out of office, Soglin has been re-elected as a self-proclaimed moderate, and David Fellman says he finally voted for Soglin for the first time. So did many real estate developers.

The current consensus is an extremely pale version of the Madison of 1950–67. I do not believe that it is just the rosy-tinted glasses of nostalgia which have caused so many who were involved to express a deep sense of loss in these retrospective essays. In microcosm—and that is what this book, true at last to its Progressive-empiricist roots, proves to be—what was tried and lost in Madison was a salient example of the best as well as the silliest political experimentation of the American left during the Cold War–Vietnam era. It was a tragedy.

GENERATIONALLY AND TEMPERAMENTALLY I was more cool jazz than rock and roll—the two touchstones James Gilbert used to described the age divide among the New Left in this book. Had I been a university freshman in 1967, that is to say if I was six years younger, I almost certainly would have been swept into direct action and, perhaps, violence. But by then I was already in my third year of graduate work at Northwestern. Although I participated in the first peace march in Chicago in 1965, and would characterize myself as having been engaged in the antiwar movement, my involvement was more in writing for an underground newspaper, *The Real Press,* and in picketing against defense employers on campus than in planning acts of resistance. I was too intellectually and ideologically detached to plunge into extreme politics, although I was there for some of the long arguments.

My most formative years of undergraduate experience had been at Oberlin College, where I was deeply affected by the civil rights movement —particularly as my father was engaged in those issues as a professor of constitutional law and a Democratic Party activist. "Blowin' in the Wind" was the perfect anthem expressing the beliefs of many. In 1963, Martin Luther King spoke at Finney Chapel in Oberlin, an experience that moved me deeply. I learned from him and from the courageous young, as well as older, black people who participated in the movement of the power of nonviolent civil disobedience as the most effective possible route to fundamental social change in the United States—an opinion I still hold. During Freedom Summer 1963, the recently deceased Alan Dawley, a friend at Oberlin and later a fine labor historian, invited me to join him writing on the *Mississippi Free Press*, but I did not come down. Ever since I have asked myself if it was essentially cowardice that kept me from making that trip, but at the time I thought that it was not my task as a northern white boy, someone who could always escape back home, to come down and tell southern blacks how to confront the brutal tyranny of segregation.

In 1963–64, the Free Speech Movement (FSM) at the University of California, Berkeley, brought the civil rights movement north, and right into universities. This was a direct transfer, as several FSM leaders, notably Mario Savio, had just returned from Mississippi and were acting as organizers for the Student Non-Violent Coordinating Committee and other civil rights organizations. Savio's speeches seemed as if they were aimed directly at my heart and head, as they did for tens of thousands of our generation of students. As the child of a liberal household, trained to be suspicious of authority, and newly transferred to the University of Michigan, an institution deeply enmeshed in Department of Defense contracts, the students at Cal articulated my alienation and my desire to resist the service university. "There's a time when the operation of the machine becomes so odious, makes you so sick at heart, that you can't take part, you can't even passively take part, and you've got to put your bodies upon the gears and upon the wheels, upon the levers, upon all the apparatus, and you've got to make it stop!" Savio proclaimed in his most famous speech during a sit-in. "And you've got to indicate to the people who run it, to the people who own it, that unless you're free, the machine will be prevented from working at all!"

The immediate issue in 1963–64 was the refusal of the Berkeley administration to permit radical organizations to distribute their literature at tables they set up on the traditionally open free-speech plaza on campus. But the critique of the modern multiuniversity quickly went deeper, into a general criticism of using education to fashion workers for industry and the military rather than to encourage social examination and spiritual freedom. Wherever that movement might have led in a peaceful world, before Lyndon Johnson escalated American involvement in Vietnam in late 1964 and into 1965, the nascent student movement, again starting in Berkeley, rapidly transformed into the antiwar movement. Particularly given the draft, which threatened our whole generation of young men, the movement mushroomed nationally—using techniques learned in the civil rights struggle grounded in moral suasion through nonviolent collective resistance.

By 1967, at Northwestern, I was engaged in research for my dissertation on American utopian communism that would lead to my first book, *The Unbounded Frame: Freedom and Community in Nineteenth-Century American Utopianism.* In some ways this was a classic New Left project, expressing deep suspicion of the nation state and all partisan-organized authorities, including the Communist Party both in the US and the USSR, as well as alienation from modern industrialization and mass society, while celebrating small, face-to-face community and individualist spontaneity. As it happened, by the time I completed the thesis I had grown suspicious of the authoritarianism inherent even in many small organizations. The tension between my communalist desires and my sense of where even progressive resisters go wrong, strengthened the study while making it a not-so-full-throated song of praise to countercultural activism.

My New Left experience was similar to that of many others. Spiritual and ideological rebelliousness in the search for authentic personal and social action trumped the desire for discipline and membership for many, probably most of us. A certain portion of the student movement proclaimed themselves Marxists—some of them actually studying Marx—and formed embryonic political parties. Others just drifted beyond traditional social mores as well as conventional institutions into life experimentation. There was a mélange of counter-cultural politics and lifestyles among which most of us moved, sampling many dishes. I was highly political and open to Marxist historical critiques, but, particularly in retrospect, I believe that I was essentially an enraged liberal who felt betrayed by the Cold War liberals who supported the escalation of the war—a group that included my own father. The generation gap was loud, angry, and all too personal for many of us.

I was attracted to the Jeffersonian, even anarchist (rather than collectivist) end of the liberal spectrum. My position on the war was that anyone who opposed it was fine with me—that I would join in any non-violent popular front activity—although I would never sign up with any party or submit myself to group discipline. At times, my comrades, both among history graduate students and in the wider New Left political world, lectured people like me for this position, insisting that if we were not part of the solution (i.e., their group) we were part of the problem. My answer drew on what the brilliant comedian Abe Burrows testified to HUAC about his Communist associates in the 1930s—that I loved to go to everyone's parties but never joined any of them. I relished argument, and my instinctive iconoclasm would only grow over the decades.

Relatively weak at Northwestern, Students for a Democratic Society (SDS), which was the largest New Left antiwar group, was headquartered in Chicago. I had several acquaintances in what became known as the "office faction," the somewhat older leadership group that tried to broaden the base of SDS by open discussion and democratic processes while maintaining a commitment to nonviolent means. (I remember one party, in a depressing cold-water flat in a white ethnic neighborhood, where I had a long, good-natured discussion with the charming SDS official who lived there about whether enduring extreme discomfort made a useful political statement or amounted to what I called "pseudo-prolitarianization.") In 1968, the SDS office faction would be glad to provoke Mayor Richard J. Daley—the Bull Connor of the North—into police riots, thus demonstrating the underlying violence of the state without initiating violence themselves. A year later, terrible debates over picking up the gun tore apart SDS and the New Left as a whole, with the younger and angrier elements, especially the Weathermen, taking over and destroying the vanguard of the student movement. Their position seemed entirely idiotic to me, as they sacrificed the moral high ground created by the civil rights and earlier student movements, choosing instead an obviously self-destructive and ugly strategy. Raging on the streets was intended to inspire black youth to revolt, they claimed. (Later, going underground and forming terrorist cells was supposed to destabilize and ultimately destroy the government by sparking The Revolution.) I remember vociferous arguments as this fundamental change was first discussed—never have I been angrier with people I knew that well. My position was simply that the state specialized in physical coercion—they had all the guns and tanks, and besides, initiating political violence would alienate almost the entire nation, destroying us as serious interveners in the American political debate. Imminent revolution was a fantasy; picking up the gun was impractical, and more importantly, an immoral means that never would lead to constructive change.

My Black Nationalist friends had their version of The Revolution, but I always thought they understood there was a considerable element of jive in their position, and we could at least communicate. The white "revolutionists," on the other hand, moved beyond discussion to self-conviction, closing ranks so narrowly that the openness and ideological fluidity of the New Left had no further meaning to them. Their perverted elitism, aided no doubt by agents provocateurs from the FBI, discredited and blew up the New Left and made a major contribution to the incessant rightward movement of American society. Gathering force after 1968 and built during Richard Nixon's divisive administration, Ronald Reagan's election in 1980 cemented the powerful Right-wing counter-revolution that swept to nearly total victory; this result was crystal clear by 1992 when I wrote this essay.

How then ought one interpret the *Sturm und Drang* of those days of New Left faith and action, knowing that the vast machinery Mario Savio urged us all to combat had regrouped to solidify not only political power but ideological and moral hegemony? Reviewing Paul Buhle's collection offered me an opportunity to reconsider intensely personal issues as well as some of the wider historical contexts in which I grew to adulthood. Most notably to me, I still felt intense anger as well as great sorrow for what had been sacrificed by the turn to political violence among my wing of my generation—the "party of change"—as Ralph Waldo Emerson labeled it long ago. And I wanted to ask about the influence of somewhat more mature members of the New Left on the younger and more violent generation. To be sure, none of the writers of these essays trashed State Street businesses or blew up math buildings. But even as early as 1967, many urged actions that would provoke violence, violence into which many of the foot soldiers were swept, and not only as victims but as increasingly vengeful and willing participants. I myself always left before the cops arrived to break heads, including at one sit-in that I had predicted in an irresponsible history lecture that could have been taken as incitement rather than mere analysis on my part. This was a serious moral issue—perhaps my anger at the rather careless apologists in this collection stemmed in part from my own sense that although deeply opposed to violence when it became an explicit policy later on, I, and those like me, had flirted with it earlier on. But then nonviolent resistance has always concerned violence; in a very real sense it plays with violence. It took great discipline to allow the government you had provoked through civil disobedience to beat on your head without firing back in order to demonstrate to the world the inner nature of the tyrannical regime you were opposing. That was the magnificence of the self-control exercised by Martin Luther King and southern African Americans of the 1950s and early 1960s, a restraint that students and northern blacks could not maintain.

So my self-doubts, combined with my sense of the ever-downward course of political change after 1968, animated this essay. Supporting civil rights for all and opposing war were noble ideals. Therefore the participation of progressives in their own demise ought not to be the cause for nostalgic celebration but for the awareness of tragedy.

Tragedy, however, is not the American Way. Knowing that, Henry James fled the country after the Civil War, a choice I understand quite well, in considerable measure from my own move so long ago to Canada. Naïve idealism is the language of mainstream American cultural and political discourse, whether coming from the Left, or, as it has for decades now, primarily from the Right. The oppositional idealism of the New Left is long gone, although many still grit their teeth and do what they can, even if only writing history essays. At my least cynical, I try to hold to what Richard Schickel described so brilliantly in the Buhle volume as the ideal of the "liberal university. [Not] grand visions but simple . . . a sense of meaning, not The Meaning."

Although thus far I have stressed something of the cultural origins and fit of the person who wrote this essay, personal memories were also central to the composition. Merle Curti was an intimate friend of our family—he was born ten years to the day before my father, both in Omaha, Nebraska, and my mother threw a lovely birthday party for them every year. Curti took me seriously from an intellectual standpoint ever since I was a boy, and his learned and engaged example had rather a lot to do with my choosing to be a historian (as did a certain nausea at the prospect of going to law school). He was a founder not merely of intellectual but also cultural and, to an extent, social history among American historians, and he was central to the group of progressive historians who made the Wisconsin department so distinctive. After reading this essay, Curti also scolded me for what I wrote about Howard K. Beale, who, in fairness, had been a racial progressive in Chapel Hill in the 1940s at some risk to himself—something I did not know when I wrote this piece.

I did not know William Appleman Williams nearly as well, although I vividly recall a conversation with him at a history conference in the late 1970s, well after he moved to Oregon State, in which he expressed deep anger for what he called the political barbarians who had destroyed his Madison. He saw his life as a painful tragedy for many reasons and expressed real regret about all the anger that his progeny had spilled onto the heads of liberals. His essay in this collection was a rather restrained version of a bone-deep hurt.

In 1981, at a Berlin conference for Fulbright fellows, I met Evan Stark, whose witty essay in the Buhle collection recalled his days as the most important student leader in 1967, when tear gas and violence first spilled over the Wisconsin campus. Stark, who had become a professor of public health in the Rutgers system, told me that he had rather admired liberals like my father, whom the students had assaulted in those days, and that he was in a sense sorry that things had spun out of control. And yet he vividly understood the young activist he had been, acting on the political necessities of the day against the war and a university administration that had supported it in effect if not in intent. His almost sweet irony, full of both regret and self-forgiveness, seemed to me about as balanced and sophisticated an approach as one could take concerning memories of such political actions. Stark had forgotten nothing, including his own complicity in events that went too far, while remembering how much further the American government was going in Vietnam.

Bearing witness can be a complex moral position. Writing in 1992, it was all too tempting to cast the first stone, and I had not been in Madison at that pivotal time and cannot say what I might have done given all the feelings and beliefs I had back then. I was there in spirit but not in body. The war in Vietnam had enraged a whole generation and any step to protest it seemed worth exploring. And yet violence was the underlying problem, a combustible force nearly impossible to contain once it was approached, and that the forces of the government truly monopolize.

Moral concerns about the meanings of political violence have remained central to my sense of self and my work ever since. Coming to terms with what unraveled in Madison was a prescient example of the problems of addressing the roots and meanings (rather than The Meaning) of political violence in American history.

2

Shadows of the Holocaust

JEWISH AMERICAN HISTORIANS AND
THE BLACK SLAVE CHARACTER

IN 1980–81, I SPENT A FASCINATING year as Fulbright Professor of American Studies at the University of Haifa. I first delivered this paper at the 1981 conference of the American Studies Association of Israel, and subsequently in Philadelphia at the April 1982 convention of the Organization of American Historians (OAH). As I sent in a solo submission, the program committee of the OAH placed me on a panel entitled "Being a Historian: Generations of Afro-American Historians." The moderator was William H. Harris of Indiana University, and the other panelists were William Banks of the University of California–Berkeley and Nell Irvin Painter of the University of North Carolina–Chapel Hill.

Later I submitted this paper to *Reviews in American History,* but that prestigious journal's editor, Stanley I. Kutler, turned it down, telling me it would get me into too much trouble. I told him I was willing to bear the risk, but that was that. I stuck the essay in a file drawer where I forgot about it until I was clearing out my office a few years ago.

"Shadows of the Holocaust: Jewish American Historians and the Black Slave Character"

When they enter the professoriat, members of various ethnic, religious, class, and gender groups of course bring their particular sensibilities, intellectual and emotional, with them into their work. Despite their fre-

This paper was first presented at the 1981 conference of the American Studies Association of Israel and later at the April 1982 convention of the Organization of American Historians in Philadelphia.

quent denials that such is the case, both in the subjects they choose and in the way they approach their subjects, scholars come equipped with subjective demands. The censorship, often freely self-imposed, of "objective" scholarship, turns work away from self-analysis, but it generally has the effect of deflecting rather than destroying the hidden agenda of the self intrinsic in the examination of others. I would urge the usefulness of developing a more conscious scholarly ethnography, a more overt approach to the links between scholar and subjects. Some cultural anthropologists have placed such analysis in their shared program. Such is not the case with historians. Here, I wish to begin an examination of the work of Jewish American historians of American history, the ethnic and disciplinary group within the world of scholarship to which I belong. I will focus on one problem as a means to approach the wider question of the links between such historians and their subjects: the means by which Jewish American historians have dealt with the question of the survival and the damage to the character of blacks under the slave regime. This particular question is not, however, chosen at random: it is central to a very lively historiographical topic, one that is especially loaded psychologically, and which arouses deeply felt debates.

Let me stress immediately that I do not mean to reduce the work of this group of historians to the elephant question. Moreover, I am well aware of the potential fuel for anti-Semites when one stresses the Jewishness of explorations of the non-Jewish world by Jews, particularly in America, where an underlying national insecurity leads to Congressional committees on *un*-American behavior. On the other hand, I am equally wary of the blindness of self-imposed censorship on this sort of topic done by Jews. Simply put, I assume that Jewishness influences the question-making processes of many Jewish scholars. This is the case despite the fact that Jewish historians of America have approached Jewish questions only indirectly for most of the past thirty years. Jews of course examine history from any number of their own perspectives—male or female, rich or poor, eastern or midwestern, and so on; they do not agree on what to interpret or how to do it; their work cuts across the American ideological spectrum. A survey of the work of Jewish American historians would nearly replicate a survey of modern history writing although there are centers of coherence, such as black history and urban and labor history. Jewish American historians, along with historians of other ethnic backgrounds, and historians influenced by their new colleagues and by contemporary events, have significantly altered American historiography in the last three decades. Very generally put (and taking into account some recent reversals of emphasis), the major shift has been away from the histories of elites and towards the histories of peoples. The base for study has been broadened, particularly in urban, social, working class, and women's and ethnic history.

It should come as not surprise that American black history, most particularly the history of slavery, is a central subject for Jewish American historians. Blacks have always been and remain the most exploited and excluded American group. Moreover, slavery has been the most dramatically brutal and unjust American institution—one that arouses the horror and empathy of most Americans, or so I would hope. It does not strike me as unusual at all that many Jewish American historians, members of another marginal group who have also been discriminated against and, in other lands, slaughtered, should identify with the struggles of black people, and should work in the field of black history. Indeed, I would argue that the Jewish enslavement in Egypt (ritually re-enacted yearly in the Passover Seder), the troubled and ambivalent history of Jewish-black relations, tensions between senses of uniqueness and desires for assimilation, and most profoundly, the Jewish enslavement and eventual extermination in World War II, have led many Jewish American historians to examine the often parallel American experience of blacks. The starkness of the oppression of American blacks evokes special responses from Jewish scholars who are at the same time reacting to the recent horrors visited upon their own people. Studying the problem of the reactions to extreme oppression among blacks redoubles, amplifies the same question among those Jewish historians who in whatever way identify with the objects of the Holocaust. It is in that sense that sometimes explicitly, more often covertly, the death camps cast their shadow on the work of many of us who in some way account ourselves relatives of the survivors of the camps.

Rather than explore the link between black slavery and Jewish American historical consciousness in breadth, I will focus on the question of the impact of slavery on the personality of the slave as raised in one book by each of two historians, Stanley Elkins and Lawrence Levine. This is the central question which each of these historians addresses directly. Elkins's book, *Slavery: A Problem in American Institutional and Intellectual Life,* published in 1959, makes an explicit and extended analogy between slavery and the Nazi death camps, and between black and Jewish psyches as fundamentally destroyed by these assertedly analogous institutions. Although the book has gone through several editions, Elkins has merely appended criticism of his many critics, much of which can be found in the collection edited by Ann Lane. He has not revised *Slavery,* nor written a subsequent book. Levine, whose book was published in 1977, partly in response to Elkins, paints a very different picture of the black slave personality. Although he does not refer explicitly to the Jews in the camps, I think that his depiction of black psyches also suggest a far different view of the psychic impact of severe exploitation of all peoples, Jews included, one built around the notions of resistance and survival. These two books which address the same question are divided not merely by the opinions or temperaments of their authors, but also by the impact of the civil rights movement, the powerful new black voices in the academy and in public life, and the cultural upheaval of the 1960s, when activism flourished in race relations, in the anti-war movement, and when concomitantly, the focus of scholarship about the responses to slavery by blacks, and also about the reactions of Jews in the camps, shifted from theories of passivity and defeat to those emphasizing energetic communal solidarity and action against the oppressor. In addition, the establishment and strengthening of the Jewish state of Israel, and the new moral opportunities and difficulties presented to Jews by this state, have also shifted the meanings of Jewish history and hence the approaches Jewish historians are likely to take concerning questions of power and powerlessness.

Elkins, writing prior to this general shift in scholarly emphasis, presumed the essentially "closed" nature of both plantation and concentration camp. To Elkins, the passage out of freedom and into slavery was total, and authority within the new system was complete; all significant authority derived from above, and the slave was a victim who internalized complete servility. Elkins's view of slavery as a closed, perfectly destructive institution has not been widely shared, although his critics will concede that he did create the agenda for that later work which attacked him. Not only has he been severely criticized, most subsequent scholarship has run explicitly counter to Elkins. Later historians have identified varieties of plantation authority, including black sources; many have stressed the strength of black religion, folk culture, family life. Also, a model of economic and political bargaining rather than brute oppression and total capitulation is now widely emphasized.

Concerning Elkins's crucial comparison, many historians have asked how analogously closed were such plantations and extermination camps. And should not distinctions also be drawn between types of Nazi camps—with the forced labor camps, and the Nazi-created ghettos seen as more analogous to plantations than were the extermination camps? Even in the latter, were not the tiniest assertions of counter-authority terribly significant to the psyches of the inmates? But Elkins's point is to demonstrate the general case, not variations: in sum and in essence he insists upon "closed" systems and "total" institutions.

If, as Elkins asserts, slavery and the death camps were closed systems, then living in such a system was, in Elkins's words, "bound to produce noticeable effects on the slave's very personality." Thus Sambo, of plantation lore, shuffles onto the stage, "docile but irresponsible, loyal but lazy, humble but chronically given to lying and stealing . . . full of infantile silliness. . . . His relationship with his master was one of utter dependence and childlike attachment." Elkins argues that this stereotype of slaves in white eyes was a correct perception of slave identity and behavior, that the closed and brutal system was sufficient to produce in general such a recognizable personality type, to "sustain infantilism as a normal feature of behavior."

With no feel for black culture, or real investigation of it, he simply dismisses it *in toto.* Instead of stressing the harmful effects of the institution of slavery (a very useful and significant point, to which I will return later), he sees psychic pulverization. His book has struck many subsequent historians, black ones especially, simply as racist. Is this so?

In fact I think Elkins's argument on blacks is premised on, not merely related to, his analysis of Jews in the death camps. Those Jews who survived for any length of time in the camps, Elkins argues, underwent total infantalization as their only means to a "full adjustment" to a closed system. "This proved possible for people in a full state of complex civilization, for men and women who were not blacks and not savages." This comparison does sound anti-black. Elsewhere in his essay, however, and primarily, Elkins is at pains to show that the devolution of rich black African cultural citizens into New World Slave Sambos was fully caused by external, environmental factors. Indeed this comparison strikes me less as an instance of anti-black prejudice than as an indirect statement of Jewish self-hatred bound to a form of survivor's guilt. It reads to me, on a subtextual level, as an anguished cry that goes something like this: "My own people collapsed in mind and soul as well as in body before the assaults of the Nazis; if they, my culturally profound brothers and sisters collapsed, how could blacks from a simpler cultural past have survived?" To my knowledge, Elkins's critics have never pointed out, from liberalism, or from fear of being considered anti-Semitic, to what extent *Slavery* is a special sort of Jewish book.

Elkins's eye-witness accounts, the data about infantilization, are drawn from the very first body of survivors' writings about the camps, many of which stressed psychic disintegration. Elkins may also have been influenced by studies of the apparently successful brainwashing of American soldiers during the Korean War, and by Erving Goffman's influential analysis of the psychological impact of "total" institutions, such as mental asylums, upon patients. Overtly, Elkins reaches his totalist psychological conclusions about blacks as well as Jews through a joining of data about camps to elements of several social psychological theories which he combines to demonstrate complete victimization—collapse in the face of unified "perverted patriarchy," finally leading to intensive identification of the prisoners with their masters, their captors.

As part of his evidence of this psychic transformation of humans into Jewish Sambos (or black-Jewish Victims, and in this book these images do meld together symbolically and analytically), Elkins cites the supposed lack of suicide, and the absence of hatred and acts of vengeance towards the SS immediately after liberation. He then quotes Eugen Kogen to make the argument that "in mass liquidations they went to their deaths with open eyes, without assaulting the enemy in a final paroxysm, without a sign of fight." Both overt, overwhelming physical dominance— the camp guards manning machine guns and electric fences—and instances of Jewish resistance, Warsaw or Treblinka, are not mentioned.

The rich, more recent literature written by survivors suggests a far more complex set of psychological processes, and much more affirmation of life in the presence of so much death than Elkins's model could suggest was possible. But what is more important in the context of my argument is that in asserting passivity at the door of the gas chambers Elkins has departed from his basic theme—the personality of the survivors for whom the camp was a perverted way of life—to the mass execution of victims. In narrative and analytic terms there is no break at all. For how many American Jews in the 1950s who survived, who entirely escaped the Holocaust personally, was the notion of supposed Jewish nonresistance a haunting theme? And if Jews could become total victims in soul and mind as in bodies, how, to repeat, could black slaves have survived such an onslaught?

On this level, the parallel between black and Jewish Sambo has a symbolically compelling quality. It remains for Elkins to make a "scientific" psychological analysis, through role theory and Henry Stack Sullivan's notions about "significant others." The servile role hinged on submission to total authority, and if that authority was the source of all possible evil, it was likewise the source of any possible good. Hence the childlike behavior, hence the never-ending search for something good in the tyrant, hence the compelling need for submission when no other stance remained plausible. And thence the "master's attitudes had become *internalized* as a part of their very selves. Those attitudes and standards now dominated all others that they had. They had, indeed, been 'changed.'" Not merely had the slave actor become a slavish personality, he had learned to love his oppressor. Elkins quotes the anthropologist John Dollard to make this final, total theoretical point. "Accommodation involves the renunciation of protest or aggression against undesirable conditions of life and the organization of the character so that protest does not appear, but acceptance does. It may come to pass in the end that the unwelcome force is idealized, that one identifies with it and takes it into the personality; it sometimes even happens that what is at first resented and feared is finally loved."

In this essay Elkins has gone all the way, as it were, in the direction of "tough-mindedness." I think this willingness on his part is what has especially provoked his critics: it also explains the undoubted power behind his essay. Jews like blacks, blacks like Jews, became slave personalities, they lost their very core of humanity, they even worshipped their own destruction. How could we Jews, we blacks have submitted? For those of us Jews or blacks who live on after this Holocaust, how dare we presume that we would have resisted and not accommodated? If they, our brothers and sisters, fathers and mothers perished in all ways, how can we know that we are alive, save by accident? We are only survivors by chance, not because of powers within our own natures. The role of slave and the alteration of an integrated, complex self into the mere shell of Sambo lurks just around Fate's previous turning, and perhaps its next. Total guilt renders wills meaningless.

For compelling reasons, Elkins thus created in the Jewish Sambo the total victim type. He was writing in the 1950s, shocked by the immensity of the Holocaust. As I have already suggested, most subsequent historiography on American blacks has argued quite to the contrary, to the point of black cultural richness and nonslavish character in the face of slavery. In the 1960s and 1970s, the social history of the dispossessed was characterized in part by a demand by historians to view their subjects in full face—up from slavery, from anonymity, from victimization—to see them as subjects and not objects. From this fine literature I have chosen as my text, Lawrence Levine's *Black Culture and Black Consciousness: Afro-American Folk Thought from Slavery to Freedom,* the book which gives the fullest single picture of slave culture. One finds in Levine's work a slave character type quite opposite that of Elkins—the almost heroic, psychologically intact member of a deep and sustaining black slave community. Whether or not Levine overcompensates in reaction to the Elkins mode of argument is a question to which I will return.

Levine opens his book with an eloquent refutation of Elkins's thesis:

> This book may dismay some because it abandons the popular formula that has rendered black history an unending round of degradation and pathology. The familiar urge to see in heroes only virtue and in villains only malice has an analogue in the desire to see in the oppressed only unrelieved suffering and impotence. This ideal construct—the pure victim—is no more convincing or supported by what we know of human psychology and history than the ideals

of pure hero or villain. To argue that in the midst of the brutalities and injustices of the antebellum and postbellum racial systems black men and women were able to find the means to sustain a far greater degree of self-pride and group cohesion than the system they lived under ever intended for them to be able to do, is not to argue that the system was more benign than it has been pictured, but rather that human beings are more resilient, less malleable, and less able to live without some sense of cultural cohesion, individual autonomy, and self-worth than a number of recent studies have maintained. Upon the hard rock of racial, social, and economic exploitation and injustice black Americans forged and nurtured a culture: they formed and maintained kinship networks, made love, raised and socialized children, built a religion, and created a rich expressive culture in which they articulated their feelings and hopes and dreams.

Levine proceeds to a brilliant and moving analysis of slave culture through careful internal examination of slave tales and slave songs, most especially spirituals. He then goes on to discuss postslavery song, folk tales, humor, and hero-figures, which lie chronologically beyond my essay. The chief point I would make about the second half of the book is, that although Levine sees continual revitalization of postslave culture he also senses a cultural declension, as black culture became less unlike white culture, once the massive, shared burden of slavery was removed, and freedmen participated, in however disadvantaged a manner, in the southern capitalist economy. If anything, to Levine, slaves had stronger links and personal characters than did the less overtly oppressed freedmen. A folk song sung by generations of blacks illustrates much of his psychological thesis:

> Got one mind for the white folks to see,
> 'Nother for what I know is me;
> He don't know, he don't know my mind.

If this song and many others like it is taken seriously, it would seem to indicate that Sambo was a self-conscious role to be played when needed, and to be turned off when not necessary. Similarly, Levine relates the recollection of a former slave who recalled that when her mistress died the house slaves paid their last respects "just a hollering and crying and holding their hands over their eyes, just hollering for all they could. Soon as they got outside of the house they would say, 'Old God damn son-of-a-bitch she gone on down to hell.'" In this incident as elsewhere, slaves judged their masters critically, they had each other, and they had their own quarters, however inferior structurally. For Levine, slavery rarely, if ever, was a total system of psychic assault. "It never pervaded all of the interstices of their minds and their culture, and in those gaps they were able to create an independent art form and distinctive voice."

Many other historians have also argued against the notion of closedness through an institutional analysis. The subterranean strength of black family and kinship ties, the bargaining involved in the exchange of labor for sustenance, and of nonrebellion for security and privacy, the variety of slave jobs, the days off and holidays, were all structural means by which the slaves participated in their own lives, rather than totally submitting to absolute authority. A model of day-to-day political exchange has proved more enlightening than a totalitarian model, even if the political participants had unequal power. Eugene Genovese, in his discussions of slave religion, and Levine in his analysis of black spirituals to my mind make a parallel and even more convincing attack on closedness by analyzing the sacred universe of the slaves. In spirituals, Levine writes, one slave might start up a new song, utilizing and transforming elements of old songs and African rhythms and motifs and then spontaneously the whole group would burst out and share the song, often in a call and response pattern. This form, artistic and social, of "almost instantaneous community" was filled with a content not of self-loathing and childishness or fantasies of catfish and watermelons, but rather with "a sense of change, transcendence, ultimate justice, and personal worth." If there were no political means to oppose slavery, there was the counter-universe of the sacred, and, "In the world of the spirituals, it was not the masters and mistresses but God and Jesus and the entire pantheon of Old Testament figures who set the standards, established the precedents, and defined the values; who, in short, constituted the 'significant others.'"

Levine does not discuss Jews or death camps, but he attacks not merely institutional closedness and the type of black Sambo, but the notion of the pure victim in general; his book is a refutation of Elkins's moral assessment. In a parallel sense, much Jewish reflection on the concentration camps has moved in the last twenty years from a focus on victimization to one on survival. Even Bruno Bettelheim, Elkins's major source and theoretician, has gradually shifted to the point where the title essay of his recent collection on the camps, *Survival, and Other Essays*, emphasized cooperation among prisoners rather than passivity or collaboration as the key to survival. I would speculate that Levine was led at least in part to his study of the strength of black personality and cultural strength by Elkins's picture of the total victim, including Jews as well as blacks. In this manner I would argue that Levine, along with many other Jewish historians of American history, myself included, implicitly more often than as explicitly as Elkins, write with the Holocaust in our minds. The Holocaust may not always be the subject of the work to which it forms an essential part of the authorial background.

Not merely does Levine write from the perspective of cultural and personality survival rather than pulverization; he emphasizes the positive aspects of slave culture nearly to the point of creating heroes. In each instance, and as a response to a general American ignorance of black culture and contempt for it, Levine emphasizes the creative communal aspect of the lives of the enslaved. If Elkins's character type, the total victim, dehumanizes blacks and Jews, Levine does tend to make near-heroes of his character type, which can also be dehumanizing in its way. If slavery was not totally closed, it often was brutal and oppressive; if black folks built a culture in the gaps of the system, if they adapted African culture to the American milieu, they also had to deal with the system itself in order to make sense of the dominant whites and of their own usually subordinate work and social roles. "Good massa" and happy slave as a plantation fiction could serve the interests of both slave and master, could even be for the slave a useful distortion and hence not totally disbelieved. If nearly all black individuals survived psychologically, they must also have been, if not pulverized, then limited, damaged. Who, black or white, Jew or Gentile, "free" or "unfree," is likely to be undamaged psychologically? What would a psychologically "whole" person possibly be like? How many people are either completely heroic or completely destroyed? What test, what character type is most human and most realistic?

Levine himself approaches material that leads to a less, nearly heroic conclusion than his analysis of spirituals and the sacred universe. The slave trickster tales he discusses at great length, though with less analytic clarity, present an almost uniformly brutal world where, by wile, the weaker animal conquers the stronger, and then destroys him mercilessly. "Vicarious triumph," rather than moral judgment, characterizes these stories, Levine concludes. In these tales, in "brutal detail the irrationality and anarchy that rules Man's universe" is depicted, a world in which "violence and duplicity are pictured as existing for their own sake." Levine has trouble squaring these very rough stories adapted from Africa and told by black slaves, with the communal warmth of the spirituals. He points to a dualistic model, where slaves had one world for themselves, and another with the whites. And yet such tales belie such bifurcation— they are as vivid and as legitimately part of black culture as the spirituals, and they certainly do not depict either solidarity or loving and undamaged personalities.

If Levine does not finally settle on a dualistic personality model, neither does he fully work out the relationship of the parts of personality presented by the tales to those of the spirituals. Put another way, he is not clear on the political, the mediating aspects of personality in the master/slave relationship. He does write at one point that these were hard and realistic stories intended for the toughening socialization of the young, a point about strategy for the survival of the oppressed that seems very sensible to me. At another place, Levine suggests that these tales were parodies of white society, with the animals serving as replicas of whites. Levine does not conclude that such conscious satire was the only purpose of the stories, and he leaves unclear the extent to which the stories also referred to the slaves themselves, and what those references might say about the slave personality. At yet another point, Levine suggests that "the slaves' interest was not always in being like the tricksters but often in avoiding being like the victims from whose fate they could learn valuable lessons." This last analysis is the softest, and the most in line with the most humane version of slave personality. But why, given extreme oppression, should most slaves *not* identify with the trickster who turns his political world upside down? Why should they not wish, at the very least in stories, harsh and violent retribution? Why should black slaves and other severely exploited peoples not lash back if and when they could? In a world where violence underlay the system and where it was frequently employed on the surface, should violence in stories indicate something other than a harsh society to which one often responded with counter-harshness, in whatever ways possible?

Indeed the trickster tales Levine utilizes read to me as cold, even frozen at the core. Such anger must frequently have been turned inward by oppressed people against their own communities, and further inwards against their own personalities, as well as in flashes outwards, in strikes at white power figures, and even in the nihilistic rebellion of a Nat Turner. All this destruction, of self, of other slaves, of the oppressor (leading back in a circle to self-destruction, as the oppressor has, by definition, a near-monopoly of the instruments of force to be used when needed), all this destruction is as undeniably part of the slave-master dialectic, and hence of the slave culture and of the slave personality, as are psychic survival and communal solidarity in the face of enormous oppression. Both inner strength and inner damage characterized slaves, who literally could not survive if they were either heroes or zombies. Of course some were heroes or zombies, but they could not survive, and most slaves did survive.

Now to be sure Levine does not create heroes in the sense that every or even many slaves were ready for the barricades, but he approaches creating slave heroes in the more limited sense that his characters were somehow more integrated and positive psychologically than seems plausible for most humans. Elkins finds, to repeat, more disintegrated and negative a personality than seems possible for slaves who, after all, somehow found the means to survive and multiply. Perhaps, in part, it is the Holocaust which makes Jewish American historians of slavery ask just this question, to push out to a less than fully human vision of interred slaves as either victim or hero, essentially intact or essentially destroyed, in the face of the oppressor. There must be, or so my speculation goes, a compelling psychological necessity within the askers of this question to push to the limits of the problem.

Many parallel questions arise from this one. What were the psychological and cultural effects of slavery and the death camps on the cultures and on the personalities of the master? Does asking this question about members of societies in extreme peril tell us anything about members of those same or other societies for whom the circumstances are less extreme? Do tests of one sort of society test the others? To what degree are we wondering about our own psychic potential when we pose this question? Most historians will bridle at this last point, as they fear above all else, the notion that history writing might be but autobiography. I would never suggest reductionism to solipsism but I would insist that history writing (as opposed to antiquarianism) is never nonautobiographical, and that personal circumstances as well as the very real sense of calling to the historian's craft of dealing with the outer, past world, characterize our work. I simply may be projecting my own Jewishness on Elkins and Levine, but I think not. They, along with others, have gone after one of the central questions about power and authority that serious-minded Jews, because of their own cultural inheritance, are obliged to raise.

Perhaps I have seemed to emphasize too much that the background of the Holocaust in some ways has limited Jewish approaches to the problems of power and authority as exemplified in the black slave character. I would wish to conclude by stressing that the depth and tensions within scholarly examinations of the slave character owe much to the compelling need to work through the terrors we have just survived, and that consciousness of the horrors of the Holocaust gives us, in fact, a great *advantage* in approaching the history of this question and history in general. And of course as all of us, Jews and non-Jews, are living in the era after the final solution, the questions I address here are part of the general agenda for historians who wish to ask questions not merely about themselves and their own culture, but also about other peoples, neither as victims nor heroes, but as humans.

IT WAS IMPOSSIBLE FOR ME to sleep the night before delivering this paper. I was to be the only white person on a panel about the writing of African American history at a time when there was considerable tension between African Americans and Jews in the historical community as well as in the wider society. And this was not my field of specialization.

As I recall it, the room was jammed—maybe it was not such a big room —but it seemed huge, and about 75 per cent of the audience was African

American. As I began delivering my argument you could hear a pin drop, and the audience remained eerily quiet while I read quite a long paper. At least that is how I remember the experience. I do recall that I had given myself a silent pep talk just before I began speaking: "You believe in this paper and these are professional historians who will give you a fair hearing. Besides, what the hell is academic freedom all about—just go for it." (Or more likely, the jauntier, "Oh, fuck it, just go for it.")

Unbeknown to me, my friend Gina Morantz, with whom I had discussed the paper, persuaded Lawrence W. Levine to come with her to the session. I had never met Larry, about whose work I was making a sometimes-critical and unorthodox analysis. After all the panelists concluded delivering their talks, I believe he rose to make the first comment, and of course, as everyone in the room admired his work enormously, they listened to him intently. As he began, I had a funny feeling that this was it for me, one way or the other. I still recall the gist of what he said; alas, he is no longer in a place to corroborate my memories, as he now lives where the choir sings spirituals and the blues whenever he wants to tune in.

"Early in my career," Larry said, in a manner I will paraphrase as well as memory allows, "in part in response to my study of William Jennings Bryan—that was my first book—Carl Bridenbaugh devoted his 1962 American Historical Association presidential address to denouncing 'outsiders' who pretended to discuss mainstream American historical figures, with my Bryan book as the primary case in point. I think that partly in response to that exclusionary anti-Semitic tirade I have tended not to think through the relationship of my Jewishness to my work. Therefore I would like to thank Michael for discussing this subject, and I think there is a lot of merit in what he says." Of course Larry was far more eloquent and fuller than that, but in any event, he set the tone for what I dimly recall as a thoughtful and calm discussion of issues of writer identity when doing history. I was so relieved; and that was the beginning of a close friendship—mind you everyone loved Larry, a big-hearted man who possessed a creative and incisive historical mind.

There is nothing like living abroad to make one sort out ones thoughts and feelings about what it means to be a North American. And in this case, there was nothing like living in Israel to push me to think not just about my American/Canadian consciousness but also my broader Jewish/American/Canadian identity. Identity is an inextricably multifaceted complex rather than an either/or, or rank-ordered collection of isolated characteristics. When you are living in the belly of your natal culture there are many identity questions that you need not ask. Of course, by 1980 I had been living in Canada for a decade and had begun questioning many of the identifiers that made me American, but I had gained no special insights into my Jewishness, in considerable measure because the place of Jews in Canadian society is generally similar to that of Jews in the United States.

Compared to Larry Levine, for example, my Jewishness was ill-informed and weakly grounded. Larry had had an orthodox religious upbringing that afforded him knowledge of Yiddish as well as Hebrew. A progressive Reform Jew, he was active in his temple and observed the holidays with understanding and joy. My father's background was similar to that of Larry. He was from a Hasidic Russian immigrant family and had supported himself through the University of Nebraska by teaching in a Talmud Torah school. But at university he rejected all religious observance, and although we were members of Beth El Temple in Madison, an extremely Reform congregation, my father attended only on High Holidays, and then grudgingly. I learned my Bar Mitzvah portion by rote and never joined a congregation during my adult life.

And yet if my family had rejected Jewish forms and ate ham (but observed the Passover Seder as a sort of ritualistic remnant whereby my father could exercise his still impressive command of biblical Hebrew), the same could not be said of Jewish values (which are of course actually Judeo/Christian). Trying to live by the Golden Rule, exercising active concern for social justice, and expressing special identification with the new state of Israel were all core family values. In addition, I learned to reject disappearance by assimilation—one should be proud of being Jewish, combat the anti-Semitic slurs that one heard even in the liberal bastion of Madison, play forward on the pretty darn good Jewish youth group basketball team, and somehow bear witness to the tragedies of Jewish history by remaining consciously Jewish. Almost all our family friends as well as my school chums and girl friends were Gentile, and we did not live a religiously separate social existence, which in any event would have been quite hard in a town like Madison—so the Jewish part of my identity was partial, and, as I look back on it, unclear.

Certainly the most painful personal experience that served in part to push me to explore the themes in this paper was a shocking and entirely unanticipated anti-Semitic attack on me in my own department at Simon Fraser University in 1972, when I was up for renewal of my contract. A young alcoholic Canadian historian of modern Germany—a Nazi apologist who wore an SS leather coat and led his students through discussions of the German decision to exterminate the Jews from the Nazi point of view—served on the elected departmental tenure and renewal committee, where he convinced all but one member, entirely without evidence, that I did not fit into the department, that I was too "cosmopolitan" (he actually used that Nazi terminology) and that my scholarship and teaching were worthless. Luckily for me, that one holdout, Don S. Kirschner, wrote a scathing dissenting brief that was sent to the dean of arts, a fine Irish poet named Dale Sullivan, who rescued me by rejecting the decision and demanding a fair rehearing. I also told my colleagues who had not served on that panel what was happening, and they helped recreate the atmosphere of decision making in the department to a certain extent. Two months later, after some change in personnel and consideration of actual data about teaching effectiveness and scholarly production, the committee reversed the judgment, with the neo-Nazi now the lone dissenter. When my renewal decision came along two years later, the dean placed Ray Bradley, a smart and tough senior member of the philosophy department, on the committee, and, with his oversight, coupled to the fact that the climate in the department had shifted sufficiently, the decision proved uneventful.

I was horrified not only that this neo-Nazi had tried to destroy my career but also that all but one of the committee members had gone along with him like "good Germans." Among other lessons, this experience proved the adage that there is nothing like anti-Semitism to make a Jew conscious of his Otherness. I did not collaborate in my demise, which is what the neo-Nazi probably expected, but fought back. Yet I was deeply and I believe permanently wounded in a way I had never been before, if in useful as well as limiting ways. For better and for worse, I toughened and grew more combative.

While I do not recall consciously using those experiences as tools of analysis, it seems clear to me in retrospect that the whole gamut of emotions I felt must have served as one more reason to explore the themes

I approached in this paper, written about eight years later. To survive, I had responded with neither infantilism nor heroism, but with anger and political tenacity. More generally, as I see it more clearly now, my worldview had darkened—never again would I underestimate the destructiveness of which individuals and groups are capable; forever would I be on the alert for the often brutal modes of domination that characterize so much of social life. My research focus began to turn from reformers to warriors and their victims.

The University of Haifa beckoned in 1980; as I learned much later the invitation came because several people in the Kibbutz Studies movement had assigned my study of utopian communism in their classes. We were keen to visit Israel in depth. My sons Joshua and Eli were twelve and seven, respectively, and they were up for adventure. By the time Josh had his bar mitzvah at the end of our stay, he understood the language he was chanting and just beamed through the ceremony. It took place not in an "official" synagogue but in a movie theater—Reform Judaism is marginalized by the theocratic elements of the Israeli establishment—in front of an almost entirely German-Jewish congregation, many of them concentration camp survivors and their children, whose openness to us was very moving.

Even for the unobservant half of the Israeli population, Jewishness was at the center of everyday life. People worked hard six days a week, and so every Friday afternoon was like preparing for a holiday—some observed the Sabbath by touring their fascinating little country by car, while others prayed and then walked down to the bottom of the road to throw stones at those passing cars. I enjoyed the disputatious serious mindedness of much of everyday life as well as the multiethnicity of Israelis. And I confess it was a real pleasure that for once Christmas was just another working day. Mind you, I had always loved singing Christmas carols and envied my friends' Christmas trees, but their absence—along with missing out on the shopping mania back home—was agreeable.

What I did not find agreeable was so many peoples' fear of Arab nations and individuals that sometimes expressed itself as racism, even on the part of many well-educated professors. "The Arab is . . ." many statements began, a classic mode of formulating hateful Otherness. This was just three years after the Camp David Accords, but many colleagues told me that one could never trust "those Egyptians," who hated Israel and would turn around and attack it when the whim struck them. I always replied that the Egyptians signed the agreement not because they loved Israel but for Egyptian reasons—to regain the Sinai and to pull out of a perpetual war that injured Egyptians. Why shouldn't raison d'etat apply to them? Wasn't Egyptian self-interest in the peace reassuring rather than fearsome? The next step in the counterargument almost inevitably referred to the Holocaust: look what happened before to judge what is likely to happen again. Never mind that the military situation was very different, that Israelis were not unarmed and dispersed aliens in Jew-hating nations committed to their organized slaughter.

I realized that this conversation was predicated on a huge wound that had occurred just prior to the founding of the new state—a state that had gathered the remnants of the death camps along with huge number of refugees essentially expelled from Arab countries. I realized that Israelis lived in the permanent and towering shadow of the Holocaust.

Although I believed (and still believe) that that mind-set, in concert with hatred and violence coming from the other side, helped to create self-destructive and frequently brutal contemporary political and military policy, I learned at the same time to understand and empathize with the fear and saw the need to explore it for myself, to deepen my own awareness of the long-term psychic wounding caused by the Holocaust. Although I cannot remember the exact intellectual linkages clearly—in part because I always have operated more intuitively than programmatically —when the Israeli American Studies Association asked me for a paper, I responded through my need to plumb the impact of the Holocaust on Jewish Americans and more specifically on my own work group, Jewish American historians. Living in Israel had brought such concerns to the forefront of my consciousness.

Because of the exciting scholarship concerning slavery during the 1970s —surely the single richest American-history specialty of that decade—I had been teaching a reading seminar on the topic at Simon Fraser. Not having the stomach to begin with the stone racist Phillips-Dunning school, I started with Stanley Elkins's book *Slavery* because it had initiated the modern study of slavery, both by its adventuresome social psychological methodology and because it so infuriated the civil rights–influenced generation of scholars that followed. Many books, including Larry Levine's *Black Culture and Black Consciousness,* were predicated on an explicit rejection of Elkins's thesis about total institutions and the obliteration of adult black slave personality. All were intent on discovering the slave community in its richness and strength, and to rescue African American history from the enormous condescension of previous generations of white scholars.

I was also fascinated by the collected essays of Bruno Bettleheim. Over a twenty-year span he had gone from his immediate postwar analysis of the slavish identification of Jewish camp inmates with the SS guards (essays that deeply influenced Elkins) to stressing fully autonomous acts of Jewish resistance in the death camps (a position congruent with Levine's approach). Bettleheim, a troubled and harsh soul, was also a social psychologist who taught a great deal to historians. Interestingly enough, as far as I discovered, he never discussed why he changed approaches.

At this time, aside from Bettleheim, I was reading quite widely in ego psychology and other forms of personality theory to try to deepen my understanding of what happens to the character and behavior of people living in extreme environments. The historically grounded work of Robert Jay Lifton, despite its heavy handed, disorganized repetitiousness, struck me as the most useful mode of social psychological analysis for historians. This reading was part of my preparation for writing not only this paper, but also my subsequent study of guerrilla warfare during the American Civil War on which I was just embarking.

Largely unremarked at the time, the majority of historians writing about slavery and African American history more generally were either African American or Jewish. (In 1986, in their excellent study *Black History and the Historical Profession,* August Meier and Elliott Rudwick would discuss this phenomenon at some length.) Beyond that observation, my essay focused on personality theory and extreme institutions. Although Elkins's likening of death camps to plantations was conceptually flawed—one place was for ruthless exploitation of labor, the other for genocide—he raised a profound question concerning psychic and collective destruction, to which Levine and many other scholars responded by stressing the powerfully affirmative communal nature of slave culture. And yet, there was a line of reasoning inherent in this revisionist work—a position with which I identified almost completely—that tended to make heroes out of humans and to eschew thorough analysis of damage to slave personalities. As I asked in my paper, who after all is undamaged? What would an undamaged personality look like? Jewish history and African American history both are tragic; tenacity and survival ought to be the causes for celebration amid the horrors of oppression rather than heroic liberationism or cultural independence, options generally unavailable in the lives of severely oppressed peoples.

Living in Israel with the survivors of the Holocaust and their children highlighted these psychological issues for me. I am pretty certain that it was there that I fully realized the Elkins book was written out of the postwar despair about the death camps, that the concentration-camp analogy came from a Jewish consciousness working through a parallel tragedy that beset black people in Elkins's American homeland. (I must note that I never met Elkins and never discussed my approach to his work with him.) Following that realization came the second one, that if spiritually Levine's book was the opposite to Elkins's, Levine, like Elkins, was not explicit about the Jewish elements of his consciousness that had done so much to propel him into his life-affirming take on slave personalities. Bettleheim provided a kind of chronological and methodological bridge from one approach to the other; his transformation was common to many Jewish intellectuals who moved from the immediate postwar discovery of the depths of the Holocaust to a fuller understanding of resistance as well as capitulation and collaboration in the camps. To a significant degree this shift was inspired and informed by the African American–generated civil rights movement, both as articulated by Martin Luther King and as lived by those brave participants in the Deep South who joyously and fearfully risked their lives in standing up against systemic oppression for their freedom. Surely this nonviolent and highly effective movement inspired a generation of Jewish American historians to identify with black history, to learn from it, and to use it in part to sort out complex feelings about the Holocaust. In retrospect, I do not think I spelled out the way in which the African American experience influenced Jewish consciousness and historical practice clearly or fully enough in my paper.

Another urgent contemporary theme behind this essay was the growing estrangement of the Jewish and African American communities. That alienation gave my paper much of its edge, and caused the sleeplessness the night before I was to deliver it. Many Jews had played prominent financial and political roles in the civil rights struggle, but the black power movement that was ignited by the wave of urban riots in the mid- to late 1960s had begun to expel white folks—many of whom were moving in a more conservative direction—from many black organizations. Many Jewish intellectuals and activists remained committed to the struggle for social justice for African Americans, while others withdrew in great unhappiness and, sometimes, anger. The most painful episode in the historical profession was the 1971 suicide of the Jewish American historian Robert Starobin in reaction to his symbolic expulsion from African American history by several black historians, an event that reverberated deeply in the profession at the time but has since been almost entirely forgotten.

Shortly before I was to deliver this paper, I recall a conversation I had with my good friend, the lively African American historian James Oliver Horton, on Jewish-black tensions. I asked Jim if he thought that both blacks and Jews laid claim to being the chosen people, and that therefore they felt a kind of competition for that communal moral high ground. Jim just laughed and said I was being way too fancy. Of course, some Jews were just white racists. Of course, some blacks were stone anti-Semites, just as were many white Christians—these were easy and common prejudices. Be that as it may, this estrangement was troubling for many Jews, and blacks as well. (On this subject Bayard Rustin in particular was eloquent and courageous.) Yet this tension, openly discussed in few scholarly settings, was yet another impetus behind my lecture. In a sense it was an accident that the paper was placed on the otherwise African American historians' panel, but this proved to be a good occasion to try to sort out the issue, not on the level of contemporary politics but on the grounds of the choice of approaches used by historians when they entered complex and contested territory.

As much as I believed I discerned a pattern in the subjectivity of Jewish American historians of slavery, I realized that my talk was highly speculative. I claimed to have discovered primary motivations for writing about slave personality that the writers themselves had not acknowledged and perhaps did not believe was true about themselves. This was, of course, one reason I was so relieved when Larry Levine affirmed that what I had said about his motivations made sense. He stressed that because of his early experience with anti-Semitic hazing he had tended to deny that his own approach as a historian differed from anyone else upholding the highest canons of the profession.

Just out of curiosity, and because he was a smart and discerning reader, I tried this paper out as well on my father, who also passed it on to a University of Wisconsin political science colleague, the late Leon Epstein, a distinguished student of British politics. Father was about twenty years older than Larry Levine, and ten years the senior of Leon. Father was a member of the first cohort of Jews to gain academic positions in the United States. Before World War II, universities were WASP bastions, with almost no members of other ethnic groups in faculty positions and with Jews consciously excluded. All the major private universities had quotas for Jewish students too. In 1934, when my father returned from doctoral work at Yale to his alma mater, the University of Nebraska, to teach, he was the second Jew on the faculty, the other being in the medical school. Although he was the most widely published scholar in his department, an anti-Semitic chairman kept him as an instructor for twelve years. (It is also noteworthy in this regard that George Mosse, the first Jewish member of the University of Wisconsin history department, was recruited in 1955.)

Both my father and Epstein quite disliked my paper. They told me that they were social scientists driven by the same imperatives as were all the members of their discipline. They had had to fight their way into the academy by upholding the objective standards of their profession even more fully than their Gentile colleagues. Their Jewishness was beside the point. Of course, I must have pushed them about the issue of denial, and neither man was an assimilationist—but they would not acknowledge that their work was driven at least in part by their Jewish identity. My father's field was civil rights and civil liberties, and he was deeply stirred by the civil rights movement, but it was simply not his style to plumb the subjective content of his work. I understood, even at the time, that what seemed to me a blind spot was in fact a product of his very real struggle to make his way in what as a young man had been a hostile environment, and so we let the matter drop.

I concluded this paper with an explicit declaration that a certain moral calling should characterize worthwhile history writing: I firmly believed that historians carry a special obligation to bear witness to the negative as well as the positive in the human experience. Historians should write to reveal harsh truths rather than to celebrate history. Now, when we live in far more ironic times, such explicit moral earnestness sounds rather dated, and I am nearly thirty years older and that much more buffeted and bruised by the complexities of living. Here and now I would be chary about expressing such values this openly lest I embarrass myself, but I would not disown the spirit of that younger man.

3

At the Nihilist Edge

REFLECTIONS ON GUERRILLA WARFARE
DURING THE AMERICAN CIVIL WAR

ONE DAY IN 1991, two years after the publication of *Inside War: The Guerrilla Conflict in Missouri During the American Civil War*, in the ancient pre-Internet era, a letter appeared in my mailbox inviting me to participate in a conference entitled "On the Road to Total War" to be held the following year in Washington, D.C., by the German Historical Institute (GHI). Intriguingly, the meeting was to be comparative in nature, dealing with the American Civil War and the contemporaneous German wars of unification.

This conference was my introduction to the excellent GHI and to the two young historians, Stig Forster and Jorg Nagler, who served as the conveners. In 1987, the German government established the American locale of the institute, which has several branches in Europe, the Middle East, and Japan, as well as in Washington. Following the same cosmopolitan inclinations that led to a united Europe and doubtless sensitive to the peculiarly destructive nature of German nationalism, several senior German historians—residing in a nation where historians are often political players of considerable stature—had pushed for the stimulation of comparative history. The German government responded not by fostering propagandistic goals (unlike the CIA when it established the United States Information Service), but by funding professional historians to conduct uncensored, cross-national, and world historical research.

Then posted to Washington as research fellows, both Forster and Nagler would later return to Europe, where Stig is now a professor at the University of Bern in Switzerland and Jorg at the University of Jena, in

Portions of this chapter first published in Förster, Stig and Jorg Nagler, eds. *On the Road to Total War: The American Civil War and the German Wars of Unification, 1861–1871.* Cambridge: Cambridge University Press, 1997.

what used to be East Germany. This proved to be the first of five conferences, collectively entitled "On the Road to Total War," that meticulously covered the ground between the 1860s and World War II. Although my area of expertise was in the American Civil War, I attended three of the later conferences to serve as a commentator from slightly outside the chronological foci of those meetings, which included late nineteenth-century colonial warfare, the two world wars, and the period between those wars. Stig and Jorg were determined to have a thorough discussion of particular topics, but they were always aware of the dangers of hyperspecialization, a form of academic narrowness to which historians are as prone as scholars in other fields.

Although most of the historians at the later conferences were receptive to unorthodox questioning, several seemed to resent the intrusion of what were to them uninformed outsiders on their turf. At times this made for lively discussions, both at the conference table and over drinks and dinner. (And two of the conferences were held in a converted monastery in a tiny Swiss village, which certainly kept us all together for four days.) I particularly recall one discussion of German military ferocity in East Africa in the late nineteenth century, during which I brought up the comparison to later Nazi behavior. A few of my American colleagues believed I was being offensive to our German hosts. However, the German historians present, understanding why I was raising the topic and long having shouldered the full burden of the history of German militarism—unlike American historians, who often avoid such discourse concerning their own nation's activities—readily engaged in discussing this line of questioning. I felt closer to them than to my fellow North Americans, on both intellectual and emotional grounds.

After I received the initial invitation, I realized that I wanted to use my paper to address several theoretical concerns stemming from my book and from the very structure of the conference. One was the human and social capacity for slaughter, considered from interdisciplinary perspectives, including cultural anthropology and social psychology, which had infused my book. Aware that I had been invited because of my work on guerrilla warfare, I wanted to test these theoretical approaches before a wider audience.

Another major opportunity was to further discussion of the necessity of doing comparative history, a proposition I thought particularly important for American historians, who tend to American exceptionalism—often premised on the notion that America is a unique City upon a Hill representing universal values—and who therefore only infrequently ask the question, compared to what? As the existence or nonexistence of the hard-to-define concept of "total war" in the American Civil War had become a staple of dispute among Civil War historians, the conference seemed an ideal place to address this idea in a comparative framework.

Most of the thirty-one papers covered either German or American topics, with the comparisons resulting from putting together two sets of historians at the same conference. The most notable exception was a fascinating comparison of Bismarck and Lincoln, tabled by the lively American historian Carl Degler, a pioneer in comparative history, whose most exceptional book in the field compares racism in Brazil with that in the United States.

Given the framework of the conference, I decided I also should try to write a paper that was internally comparative. Although I had done no research on the English Civil War, which served as one of my comparisons, I could of course read in the vast literature of that field for myself. And Oliver Cromwell was a cousin to the American Puritans—his militant Protestant ways of thinking were not entirely alien for an American historian.

The Thirty Years' War, which I also discussed, was more of a reach, as I neither spoke nor read German and had to depend on secondary sources written in English concerning a topic three hundred years prior to my area of specialization. As I suspect is the case for many historians when considering such distant but immense mountains, I felt insecure and inadequate to the field of study. But I decided to bull ahead, both to challenge myself and in recognition of the fact that few professional historians are fully equipped to do comparative history, and that therefore little such work is attempted. Given the setting of the conference, I wanted to address a subject in German history that related to my interest in the brutal experience of massive irregular warfare in the American Civil War. This comparison struck me as of explanatory value, and I reckoned others could set me straight about the mistakes I was making.

Also, on the face of it, the very title of the conference provoked me. "On the Road to Total War" was a paradigm premised on modernization theory, about which I harbor grave doubts. I do not think history is linear, nor do I believe that progressive chronological determinism explains as much about the destructiveness of wars as do cultural factors that license and limit violence. Hugely destructive war is not a modern development. Therefore, I took it as my task to counter the unintended but not infrequent scholarly tendency to reduce the horrors of the war experience through creating a distancing master narrative. I would try to understand armed conflict as a pragmatist, in the concrete circumstances in which it occurs. Writing comparative history drawn from different times and cultures that nevertheless demonstrates certain shared characteristics, can lead us to a deeper understanding of the impulses and practices of war than can an abstract developmental model. Or so I believed. This set of reactions to the central premise of the series of conferences drove my paper as well as my participation in later years.

"At the Nihilist Edge: Reflections on Guerrilla Warfare during the American Civil War"

As defined in our times, total war is a twentieth-century outcome of twentieth-century capacities for social mobilization, ideology, and technology applied to war-making ends. What looks, in certain respects, like its predecessors, such as the American Civil War and the German Wars of Unification, prove on closer examination to be markers on an undulation in levels of wartime violence reaching far back into the history of warfare, rather than developmental stops on a simple linear and progressive development of modern war that culminated during the twentieth century.[1]

Many "premodern" wars reached horrific levels of destruction. Perhaps the most dramatic example of a much earlier war that reached a far greater level of violence than did those of the 1860s was the Thirty Years' War, which destroyed much of Germany during the period from 1618 to 1648.

> The story in the reports is repeated a hundred times: the bands of mercenaries destroyed domestic utensils, tools and furniture, ruined stores and seeds, slaughtered or took away cattle and the domestic animals, inflicted cruel tortures on the inhabitants or killed them

and set fire to the farm. . . . This was expressly forbidden by all the rules. In addition, it also frequently happened that young plants and ripe corn were deliberately trampled down by the armed plunderers or military detachments on the march and not without the senseless killing of the village inhabitants either. It is likewise occasionally reported that the healthy and able-bodied inhabitants were driven away and sold . . . for eternal labor, far worse than death.[2]

In this instance of war against all civilians, the purchasers were Turks, the enslaved inhabitants German peasants, the sellers Swedish invaders. During the Thirty Years' War, waves of foreign troops, Danes, French, Spanish, and especially Swedish, invaded the disorganized Holy Roman Empire. Linguistic and ethnic hatreds multiplied religious conflicts between Catholics and Protestants; invading soldiers and local rulers alike also despised, exploited, and slaughtered the German peasantry peopling the countryside through which all the armies marched. "When the German peasants [of Brandenburg-Kulmbach] attempted to drive out the [Swedish] invaders, in November, 1631," Geoffrey Parker writes, "they were massacred: a chronicler who visited the site of the peasants' last stand was appalled to find the vineyards and fields red with blood, with corpses scattered in bizarre positions over a three-mile radius."[3]

Horrendous as were these invasions of organized armies, even more profoundly destructive were the freebooting actions of marauding mercenaries, most often foreigners, who were demobilized each winter, without pay, but with their arms, the better to prey, in the name of foraging, on villagers and peasants. By the war's end, in Rhineland-Lauten, thirty-six of sixty-two towns were deserted, while the chief town of Kaiserslautern had dropped in population from 4,200 to 500. The peasants fared the worst—when not raped and murdered, they were, even more frequently, plundered and burned out of home and crops and left to wander or to camp unwelcome in towns where they faced malnutrition, which vastly increased rates of death by typhus, dysentery, and bubonic plague while lowering birth rates. In many places, the war was such as to inspire Thomas Hobbes. One village near Nuremberg was plundered eighteen times in two years. Peasants organized guerrilla forces of their own to counterslaughter the mercenaries when opportunities arose, but more

often, the outgunned peasants died or fled. Desperation induced all in-
humanities, cannibalism included.[4]

Coolly discussing death rates rather than terror, modern historians
of the Thirty Years' War have fully debated the probable level of the deci-
mation of the German population by violence and by epidemics. Conservative estimates are that "only" 3 or 4 million of the 20 million Germans
alive in 1626 died or were killed during the war. Even by these cautious
reckonings, between one-half and two-thirds of the people of Mecklen-
burg, Pomerania, and Württemberg perished.[5]

As the Thirty Years' War demonstrates, if the central test of the level
of destructiveness reached during war is the degree of erasure by soldiers
of the discrimination between combat and civilian, then nothing was
new about the behavior of German or American troops in the wars of
the 1860s. That is an understatement. Although there were episodes in
the Civil War and the German Wars of Unification that paralleled those
of the Thirty Years' War, neither approached the general level of human
destruction of that earlier conflict. Indeed, one can discover episodes of
massive military destruction of civilians in the military behavior of the
first so-called Western civilizations. The slaughter or enslavement of enemy civilians, and the destruction of their home fields and home cities,
was common wartime practice among the Greeks and Romans and their
competitors.

Conflating the scale of war with the modernization of war is anachro-
nistic not only in mismeasuring the ebb and flow of slaughter during the
long history of armed conflict; it also distorts the contemporaneity of the
ability to wage total war. Rather than growing directly from earlier wars,
the twentieth-century meaning of total war owes more to the pen of
General Erich Ludendorff, whose 1935 book, *Der Totale Krieg*, suggested a
mass economic and social mobilization, such as was approached by Nazi
Germany, but only in 1944, guided by Albert Speer.[6] Beyond Ludendorff-
style total social and economic mobilization and newly available techno-
logical advances such as those that allowed massive strategic bombing in
World War II, the systematic ideological dehumanization and thorough
bureaucratization achieved by the Nazis in their slaughter of six million unarmed Jews, killed as a purely civilian category, form parts of the
contemporary meaning of total war. In addition, the full contemporary

meaning of total war is predicated on the omnipresent fear of the annihilation of the entire human race by nuclear war, for which the Americans provided the horrendous test cases at Hiroshima and Nagasaki. Roman swords, not to mention seventeenth-century muskets, were sufficient to produce a level of slaughter of civilians not much improved upon prior to 1945, and nuclear weaponry has proven to be so globally threatening that it has thus far remained unusable, leaving killing to the old-fashioned weapon systems. Modernization theory will not go far in explaining thresholds of violence, either observed or crossed. Not technology, nor thorough organization, but cultural factors have always determined the level of slaughter and restraint from slaughter in war—"totality" linked to "modernization" are just historians' words, as the marauding mercenaries and peasants fighting in Germany well realized 350 years ago.

If chronological progressivism and modernization theory distort far more than they illuminate, how then can we understand this seemingly arbitrary record of greater and lesser intensities of warfare over the centuries? One crucial variable is what one might call the cast of the cultural net: the treatment accorded by warriors to those whom they consider to fall inside their culture as opposed to the treatment that they apply to those whom they consider to be cultural outsiders. Consciously or unconsciously, warriors of all nations apply their cultural standards while at war. In addition, their level of cultural inclusion and exclusion and of destructiveness is amplified by the form of combat in which they engage. Irregular warfare, where formal command structures are weak or absent, frequently has provided fertile grounds for the most devastating enactment of war against the people, restrained by the fewest cultural inhibitions.

During the American Civil War, the military theater most nearly approximating that of the marauders and peasants of the seventeenth century was in the hill country of the border states and the up-country South, where guerrilla war broke out spontaneously between local communities internally divided between Union and Confederate sympathies. In some areas, particularly in up-country North Carolina and East Tennessee, Unionists took to the bush to fight a guerrilla war against Confederate troops, while in other areas, particularly Kentucky and Missouri, young men of Confederate leanings banded together to fight Union authorities. Although I know most about Missouri, from which my primary evidence is drawn, most of the phenomena found there were replicated elsewhere in the warring border regions. If all war is the application of collective violence with implicit and explicit limitations, the guerrilla war was, owing to its fundamental disorganization, the locale with the fewest explicit limitations during the Civil War. The tendency toward indiscriminate slaughter of an enemy's civilians as well as of its soldiers, present in all wars (and perhaps in the human breast), and the infatuation with nihilism, both found their fullest but by no means exclusive play in the guerrilla aspects of the Civil War.[7]

Pro-Confederate guerrillas in Missouri formed not in regular units, with uniforms and flags waving, but in temporary small bands, in ordinary clothes, gathering in secret places, and then striking out with stealth and bursts of violence at the Union enemy or at whom they deemed to be the enemy's civilian supporters, thence dispersing to melt back into the civilian population. Union troops could not discern which among all those smooth-talking civilians actually were deadly guerrillas or guerrilla sympathizers, and badly frightened and furious over the loss of their comrades' lives, they therefore tended to strike out blindly at anyone who seemed threatening or untrustworthy to them. This shared dialectic of negation created a cycle of destruction, where justice came to mean vengeance, where one death was to be answered by ten retributive killings, and ten by a hundred. Over four years, perhaps ten thousand Missourians were killed this way and perhaps three hundred thousand (of 1.2 million) fled their homes for the relative safety of Union garrison towns, or for more distant and safer cities, leaving behind burned homes and fields, slaughtered livestock, bands of wolves, and armed marauders of both political persuasions.

Both sides adopted a slash, burn, and kill policy. Pro-Confederate guerrillas operated on their own, far from Confederate military or civilian control. On the other side, although some legal controls remained in civilian hands, most Union authority in the ravaged countryside devolved into military hands—the Provost Marshal at the local outpost exercised such police authority as remained in rural areas often dominated by enemy guerrillas.

General Union policies varied wildly—war taxes and land confiscation, loyalty oaths, banishment or jailing of known (or more often suspected) civilian guerrilla supporters, all proved ineffective and were applied unevenly or abandoned outright. In the most dramatic incident of this long and formless conflict, after a guerrilla raid on Lawrence, Kansas, on August 21, 1863, in which at least 150 unarmed civilian men and boys were executed, the Union general in Kansas City issued a general order depopulating the four Missouri counties from which the raid had been staged. Approximately twenty thousand civilians of all political persuasions were forced to vacate their homes and lands, all of which then were torched. These four burned-over counties were a sizable chunk not of a Confederate but of a *Union* state, and this undiscriminating official attack on all civilians, including Unionists, and on women and children as well as men, produced such an outcry all over the North that this extreme policy was quickly withdrawn, never to be repeated. This revocation demonstrated the cultural and political limits imposed by American public opinion, expressed through a free press, even in the midst of a civil war, against the potential application of draconian antiguerrilla policies to civilians and their property.[8]

All other Union antiguerrilla policies were less sweeping, but all suffered from the fundamental impossibility of distinguishing guerrillas from civilians, and enemy from friendly civilians. While in command in Missouri early in 1862, General Henry Halleck had issued a general order that captured guerrillas be shot summarily rather than being taken prisoners of war. After he went to Washington as general in chief, Halleck commissioned Francis W. Lieber, a German-American legal scholar, to draft what became General Order no. 100—the application of martial law to guerrilla-infested regions. Guerrillas, Lieber wrote, were "not entitled to the privileges of prisoner of war, but shall be treated summarily as highway robbers or pirates." Likewise, civilians who guided guerrillas or gave them military information were "war traitors" whose punishment was to be death. On the other hand, Lieber's orders insisted that sheer military tyranny was wrong, that every commander "who possesses the power of arms against the unarmed" had for that very reason to be "strictly guided" not by "cruelty but by the principles of justice, honor, and humanity." The honorable commander thus would treat enemies with summary execution, and all others with justice.[9]

Of course, only the most Solomonic commander could have distinguished his enemies from innocent bystanders in the deep haze of guerrilla war. In the fury of action, it often proved impossible to determine which execution was just and which arbitrary, and, after the bloody deed had been done, mere suspicions were easily enough rationalized as having been real threats. Union commanders in the field, urged on by their men as well as by their own fear and anger, tended therefore to shoot when in doubt. In practice, neither side took many prisoners—the torch and immediate capital vengeance were the norm.

It was the brutal guerrilla slaying of one of his men that led General Samuel R. Curtis, a West Point man, to his no-prisoner stance. He wrote to St. Louis headquarters in May 1862, that "a set of assassins are prowling about Little Red River. One of our men bathing in that river was shot down and beaten to death with clubs. I have ordered such villains not to be taken as prisoners." Curtis was far from alone in his willingness to declare openly to headquarters such a no-prisoner policy. "We take no prisoners," Col. James Ford wrote to St. Louis in 1864. Such officers instructed their men to show no quarter. Private George Woltz wrote to his parents from southern Missouri in 1864, "there are strict orders against taking any more prisoners that is found in arms or as bushwhackers but to leave them on the ground we found them on." Nevertheless, guerrilla prisoners sometimes were taken because shooting disarmed enemies in cold blood was morally too much for some Union troops. Such hesitancy could annoy commanders such as Colonel Bazel F. Lazear, who responded to the capture of the guerrilla chieftain Bradaway and several of his men, "I am sorry that they are prisoners on my hands, as they should have been shot on the spot." In such instances, a no-prisoners policy for guerrillas could be rendered somewhat more "legitimate" through a quick kangaroo court. For example, William C. Long wrote to his children from the field in 1862, "we captured a bushwhacker yesterday. . . . He has been tried by drum-head court-marshall [sic] and condemned to death. He will be executed in about one hour. His grave is now digging." A widely used formula allowing for an even quicker quasi-moral execution was expressed by Union Cavalry Captain Thomas Thomas, in his official report from the Ozarks in 1864 concerning the capture and fate of Jacob Rustin and John Inman, two "notorious bushwhackers. On the march to camp the prisoners attempted to make their escape by running, and both were instantly killed."[10] This common formulation provided safety against possible official recriminations as well as psychological defense for the executioners against the nakedness of committing outright murder.

Guerrillas reported to no one but littered the countryside with the corpses of their enemies whom they executed as they would be executed. Not merely did both camps of fighters kill one another; they frequently scalped and otherwise mutilated the bodies of their murdered foes. Fighters took body parts—ears, noses, scalps, teeth, facial skin, fingers—to keep or give away as trophies. On September 14, 1864, Major Austin King's command killed five of the notorious Bill Anderson's men, "some of their bridles being decked with human scalps." Two months earlier, Archie Clement, by reputation the leading executioner in Anderson's gang, had attached a note to the remains of a Union soldier, which proclaimed proudly, "You come to hunt bushwhackers. Now you are skelpt. Clenyent skelpt you."[11]

Union troops doubtless reciprocated in kind, but as the victors purged the records, little direct evidence of their mutilations remains. Something of Union fury toward the enemy can be recaptured in the order that General Clinton B. Fisk gave to a Colonel of his command on April 16, 1864, "Try the bushwhacker by drumhead court-martial tonight, and let every soldier in Macon shoot him if he is guilty, as he doubtless is."[12] One bullet, or at most a firing squad, would have sufficed; Fisk prescribed collective, ritualized dismemberment. Killing the enemy was incomplete; one had to finish the dehumanization, literally deface the enemy, by rending his flesh, which somehow contained his evil soul. Drenched in the endless terrors of a guerrilla war, combatants sought release in the obliteration of the face of the Other. Some guerrilla warriors wished to push on toward a place of total destruction, some land where "we" in all our force are all and "they" are rendered into nothing at all. Each side could seek this end for their enemies, as each knew they had been targeted. This urgent, two-way, furious desire amounted to a mutual aesthetic of destruction, placing the fighters at the edge of the nihilist abyss, their repellent and attractive genocidal dreamland.[13]

Surely the likes of Bill Anderson and Clinton B. Fisk were psychologically equipped to have replicated the full experience of central Germany centuries earlier. And yet, horrendous as was the guerrilla war in Missouri, it stopped short of the level of destruction and slaughter reached in that earlier conflict, in part because people on both sides had so much in common. In Missouri, there was no arrogant aristocracy that observed the poor as a less than human subspecies of peasants, who were subject to separate and unequal laws and social consideration. Then, too, the combatants, 90 percent of them, shared the Protestant faith. There were both northern and southern branches of the dominant Baptist and Methodist sects, but all shared a basic pool of religious practices and values. Ninety percent of Missourians were small landholders or aspiring tenant farmers. Only 10 percent of these held slaves, and then only small groups of slaves, unlike the huge gangs of slaves characteristic of slaveholding in the lower South. The issue of slavery divided the state, of course, although the Confederate party was far larger than its slaveholding leadership. Seventy-five percent of Missourians on both sides were "Butternuts," descendants of Anglo-Saxon migrants from the upper South. Racially, ethnically, linguistically, religiously, and economically, in terms both of livelihood and of aspirations, the vast majority of Missourians of both political persuasions were cut from the same cultural cloth.[14] Their brutal war was not a war of religion, nor a class war, nor a war of race or ethnicity. Although impossible to document conclusively, these absences of fundamental social fissures both lent special horror to what really was a brother's war, and served to limit the full-blown dehumanization necessary to something more nearly approaching a genocidal Armageddon.

In addition to sharing a pool of demographic, economic, and social characteristics, fighters on both sides shared fundamental cultural values. Although wildly distorted by the lying and violence that they inflicted upon one another during war, they also clung to at least vestiges of their peacetime values, perhaps to prove to themselves that they still retained their core personalities and their membership in what they thought to be the human family. These were Evangelical Christians, American republicans who shared the egalitarian belief that each individual ought to be free and freely respectful of the personhood of others. They also shared values of honor—that a man (or woman, though here the male fighters and hence masculinity are more to the point) ought to be forthright with others while defending the integrity of his person and his family through mutual fellow-dealing at best, and fair fighting at worst. Most especially, the honor of men was tested by their protective attitude toward the weak, especially the elderly, women, and children, the necessary complements to themselves in the proper family, which was the indispensable core unit of their otherwise lightly institutionalized society, the central building block of their culture. By extension, fighters on each side sought to preserve not only their own women, children, and families, but the abstract principle of loyalty and service to kinship, represented by their own families, yet equally embodied in other families like their own. Even when they maimed and killed one another, men did so in perverse testimony to these core values.[15]

The clearest demonstration of male service to the code of honor was the manner in which women understood the verbal and behavioral latitude that men afforded them, even while they slaughtered one another. Iowa Private Dan Smith wrote back home about his responses to the "rampant secesher" women of Boonville. "They said the Iowa boys conducted themselves more like gentlemen than any other troops that had been here. The women were the spunkiest I ever seen and when a squad of us would visit a house we would have to take a few broadsides but our orders were to do things as civil as possible but I felt several times like if I could see them strangled." Smith's reactions to the traitorous Boonville women were complex. He admired their sauciness (which he would never have taken off enemy men) and also the gentlemanly reflection he sometimes saw coming back from their eyes, but he also held a partially acknowledged homicidal fantasy toward them—expressed, however, only in the passive voice. His peacetime sense of gender proprieties, and that of the Boonville ladies, was stretched but not broken under guerrilla war duress.[16]

Union Captain Edwin F. Noyes reported his much angrier and surlier reaction to a similar scenario early in the war. When he requested water for his thirsty troops, one Missouri woman had said that she would not give a drop to his "beer-swilling, nigger loving, cowardly dogs to save their lives." Noyes had replied to the woman "you are a woman: if you were a man, we would have an answer in our guns."[17] Unlike Private Smith, Captain Noyes was not even partly amused; neither, however, did he pull his trigger. His foul-mouthed enemy knew to what extent her gender lent her immunity, even during military action.

Confederate guerrillas observed the same limits of attitude and behavior toward women, and whereas there was a Union command structure to reinforce the forbearance of Union soldiers, the guerrillas had none—they restrained themselves in service to implicit cultural constraints not reinforced by external institutions. Sometimes even the most brutal of guerrillas in the middle of bloodbaths would stop to observe the cultural ban on directly harming women. To give one horrendous example, on the night of May 6, 1865, Mrs. Mary Hall was awakened by a group of guerrillas. They demanded she light a candle and then took it and set light to her children's clothes, shoving them under the bed where the three children were sleeping. "I caught the clothes that were burning and threw them in the fire place. One of them says [']God damn you let them; if you don't I will burn up the house.['] I answered they will burn just as well where they are and will give more light." They then went to the bed of her eighteen-year-old son and demanded his pistol. He said he had traded it for a watch and added, "its hanging by the glass though some of you have it—as I do not see it. One of the guerrillas then said god damn him. Shoot him. I thought they would shoot him and knocked up the pistol several times, injuring my shoulder by so doing," Hall reported. "They finally succeeded in shooting him in the head killing him instantly. I was screaming and entreating them all the time to spare his life. After they had killed him one of they says shut your God damn mouth or I will blow a hole through you head. . . . All this time my niece, 16 years of age was lying in bed. One of the guerrillas stood by her bedside and as she made an effort to rise ordered her to lie still saying one woman was enough at a time. After they had killed my son and plundered the house one guerrilla ordered me out of the house and shut the door. The door had scarcely closed before I heard my niece scream and say Lord Aunt Mary run here to me. I started and as I reached the door my niece who had succeeded in effecting her escape from the men came rushing out. I says let the poor girl alone you have done enough. . . . I do not think they effected their designs on the girl."[18] Mary Hall could not protect her son from slaughter, but she could aid in preventing her niece's rape, mainly because the guerrillas were unwilling to complete a rape under even these circumstances. The assault went up to the edge of rape and murder of women. This was the most negative version of the observation of the code of protection of women.

Part of the perversity of armed chivalry was the God-like power it gave the warrior over the fate of women. In their moments of armed domination, guerrillas had the power to do what they alone willed, including murder; thus withholding destruction could also give them an enormous sense of potency. During the Lawrence raid, two guerrillas had their pistols drawn on Henry Bissell, when his pretty sister Arabella, according to a later report by their mother Sophia, began "pleading . . . with the leader to spare her only brother, running from him to the other and back again in agony. The leader relented and spoke to the man. He let go his hold, and Henry ran for corn. . . . They tipped their hats and bid me good morning."[19] Such an incident no doubt heightened the self-image of the gentleman for these two guerrillas; it was a demonstration of their total power over Arabella, even more than over Henry, who in this situation would have had no effective means to plead for himself.

Many on the Union side attested to this guerrilla maintenance of the manly code. An Illinois journalist wrote during the worst summer of the guerrilla violence around Independence: "In this country the old notion that men are the protectors of women has exploded, the tables are turned, men are now the weaker vessels, and women the protectors. A man dare not travel five miles from Kansas City, but with his wife he feels comparatively secure. Bushwhackers have not yet raised a hand against a woman, they sometimes burn a house over her head but are careful not to injure her person."[20] In fact, customary deference had been twisted into a power game between men who could proclaim that their slaughter of one another was done in service to their protection of women.

At least the occasional warrior was conscious of the weird mutation of the male code prescribing the proper treatment of women that he had adopted during the guerrilla war. Discussing his self-awareness during a typical search of a suspected guerrilla lair, inhabited only by women, Lieutenant Sardius Smith recorded one night in his diary, "We are getting quite hardened to this kind of thing and can go into a house with a pistol in my hand, with a smile on my face, speak politely to the ladies, ask where their men are in order that I may shoot them with as much grace as though I was making a call for friendship sake."[21]

However partial, however selective was its observance, the male code of honor continued to limit some aspects of masculine behavior during the guerrilla war, even while serving to license other outbreaks. What one sees in action are cultural inhibitions intertwined with cultural licenses, combining to create a nastily dynamic dialectic. Destructive impulses most often overrode peacetime reserve, especially when groups of young men attacked other groups of young men, but the code of honor, strangely reworked and sporadically reasserted, served to dampen somewhat the rush toward total destruction.

Vestiges of honor applied only to those whom the warriors considered to be within their cultural net. The exclusion of people as the Other, as anti-beings, eliminated almost all inhibitions for these same fighters. During the Civil War, as has been generally true in the history of the United States, those Others have been defined by race. In Europe, class and ethnocultural divisions, which had none of these nihilistic consequences during the American Civil War, had justified, as they still do, slaughters at least as apocalyptic as those that nineteenth-century Americans enacted on the racial Others.

The code of honor, this marginal reticence, applied in the American guerrilla war only to white women and white families. Indeed, there is evidence that German American men, who were nearly all Unionists and recent immigrants, never were spared by Confederate guerrillas and were strung up or shot with special glee. Even if Germans were feared and loathed as aliens by Anglo-Saxon Missourians, however, there is evidence that German women were spared rape and murder. A common race, differing ethnicity notwithstanding, placed Germans at least tentatively within the recognized racial community, marginally inside rather than outside American culture.[22]

Unlike German women, black and Indian women lived below the racial pale—the code of honor did not apply to them. Many black women were abused, beaten, and raped during the war as they had been during slavery times. Escaping slave women who attached themselves to Union armies found in their newfound freedom that Union soldiers took up much of the physical tyranny of their former owners. One explicit example of rape in the Missouri guerrilla war context comes from the testimony of Francis Kean at the court-martial of guerrilla James Johnson. Kean testified that Johnson and two other bushwhackers had seized her eighteen-year-old slave girl. "They rode on a piece and said to her, 'God damn we will punish you. . . .' Johnson then got off his horse and said now ride boys and she told me they all done with her what they wanted to—she said they violated her person." In March 1864, a slaveholder named Tapley of Pike County recaptured his escaping slave woman. As she refused to tell him where she had hidden her three children, she was, an unsigned letter to the *Chicago Tribune* later reported, "stripped and beaten on the bare back with a band saw until large blisters formed, and the wretch sawed them open, under which treatment the poor woman died."[23]

The most horrendous example of the general violation of nonwhite women in Missouri was the Sand Creek, Colorado, massacre of a peaceful tribe of Cheyenne Indians on November 19, 1864. The extermination of about five hundred Indians, mainly women and children, took place west of Missouri, but socially similar Union volunteers carried it out. A sickened young officer, who came from New Mexico but was temporarily attached to the Colorado militia, later reported that in addition to the widespread shooting down of fleeing women and children, he saw widespread mutilation of them. "I also heard," James D. Cannon reported, "of numberless instances in which men had cut out the private parts of females and stretched them over . . . their hats while riding in the ranks."[24] The guerrilla war in Missouri, of whites against whites, never crossed these barriers.

Not merely in the guerrilla war or in Indian warfare did white soldiers treat other races by significantly lower standards than they treated enemies of their own race. As opposed to the no-prisoner policy among white fighters in Missouri, elsewhere regular armies on both sides were nearly always scrupulous about taking prisoners rather than shooting them summarily, treating others as they would wish to be treated. However, this military and cultural inhibition of slaughter did not apply to the treatment accorded by Confederate captors to black Union prisoners, particularly in the western theater. On April 12, 1864, screaming "No Quarter!" and "Kill the damn niggers, shoot them down!" Confederate troops under the command of the renowned General Nathan Bedford Forrest overran Fort Pillow, Tennessee, and, following Forrest's orders to shoot them down like dogs, massacred over one hundred blacks who had surrendered, burying some alive, setting fire to tents containing wounded blacks, shooting four little boys and two black women and throwing their bodies in the Mississippi River. That same month, other Confederates under General John S. Marmaduke, a well-bred Missourian, executed a perhaps larger number of black prisoners at Poison Springs, Arkansas. Subsequently, black soldiers sometimes would murder Confederate prisoners, shouting "Remember Fort Pillow!"[25]

White Confederate and Union soldiers generally regarded decent treatment of prisoners of war, even those taken immediately after the killing of their squad mates, as a mark of manly honor, thus demonstrating their subscription to rules of a fair fight, which they did not extend to black soldiers. At those moments when the Civil War was also a race war, the different rules that applied lowered the threshold of legitimated violence. When the fight was between white Americans, soldiers generally were willing to limit their killing in combat, not because they lacked firepower or because of tactical shortcomings, and not just because their officers enforced restraint, but primarily because they continued to act at least in part within the restraints of their implicit, shared moral code.

If the guerrilla war theaters of the Civil War provided a brutal testing ground of the tension between approaching nihilism and preserving cultural and personal inhibitions, the psyche of Gen. William Tecumseh Sherman provided another key venue of inner conflicts, both acted out and constrained. Sherman was the representative man of the western war; he was lean, hard, mean, and relentless. He had been deeply affected by the guerrilla war that he had seen when he was posted in Missouri early in the conflict. He was bright, sometimes depressed, sometimes manic, endlessly and carelessly garrulous about his feelings as well as about his opinions, and he transformed himself into a fighting leader beloved to his men and hated as the devil incarnate in the South. During his incendiary march through Georgia and the Carolinas, he not only trailed destruction but all the while gleefully proclaimed his mission to destroy the very soul of the Confederacy. This self-declared grim reaper transformed himself into the implacable embodiment of the Union war against the South.

The argument over whether or not the Civil War was a total war often focuses on assessments of Sherman's intentions and activities. The Atlanta Campaign, the inexorable march through Georgia to the sea at

Savannah and then up through the Carolinas, burning a broad swath through the countryside and the cities, without doubt were intended by Sherman to break the fighting spirit of the southern rebels. Sherman succeeded. Lest any Confederate miss the point of his actions, Sherman also loudly advertised the meanings of his campaigns, which he clearly realized to be psychological even more than military events. On the eve of the march from Atlanta to the sea, Sherman wrote to Grant, "If we can march a well-appointed army right through [President Jefferson Davis's] territory," we will make "a demonstration to the world, foreign and domestic, that we have a power that Davis cannot resist. . . . Thousands of people abroad and in the South will reason thus: If the North can march an army right through the South, it is proof positive that the North can prevail in this contest, leaving only open the question of its willingness to use that power . . . I can make the march and make Georgia howl!"[26] The last part of this letter, because of its pungent phrasemaking, is the best remembered. Even more chilling than the authentic anger of the letter, however, is Sherman's cool calculation of the impact that a campaign of organized terror would have on the South.

Six weeks earlier, when he had been shelling Atlanta, which the Confederates had turned into an armed fortress with civilians living inside, Sherman traded invective with Confederate General John B. Hood, who condemned Sherman for his "studied and injurious cruelty," which was the worst ever in "the dark history of the war." Rejecting Hood's charges as they applied to Atlanta in particular, Sherman accepted them in general. Sherman wrote to Hood:

> You cannot qualify war in harsher terms than I will. War is cruelty, and you cannot refine it; and those who brought war into our country deserve all the curses and malediction a people can pour out. . . . You might as well appeal against the thunderstorm as against these terrible hardships of war. They are inevitable, and the only way the people of Atlanta can hope once more to live in peace and quiet at home, is to stop the war, which can only be done by admitting that it began in error and is perpetuated in pride. . . . I want peace, and believe that it can only be reached through union and war, and I will conduct war with a view to perfect and early success. But then my dear sir, when

your peace does come, you may call on me for any thing. Then will I share with you the last cracker, and watch with you to shield your houses and families against danger from every quarter.[27]

Sherman's rhetorical purpose was clear—he was after not only the material but, even more significantly, the moral and emotional center of the Confederacy. He did not burn all of the South, which he could not have accomplished even if he had wished to do so. But he wanted to make an explicit demonstration that he could burn it piece by piece if this proved necessary, and he also wanted to show that he had the necessary destructive energy to accomplish whatever was required. Not only did Sherman write this message; he broadcast it to the people, South and North. A well-known hater of the press and a reactionary antidemocrat in many ways, Sherman also understood the necessity of reading the hearts and minds of the people, which, owing to the newly available telegraph and high-speed, cheap newspaper technology, were available to him. Sherman seized hold of the new technology in an effort to subdue the rebellion. In propagandistic abilities, Sherman was indeed the first of the modern generals. And in his equally acute consciousness of the impact of terror on civilians, proclaimed as loudly as possible, Sherman was also a powerful psychological warrior of a kind that we usually associate with twentieth-century military leaders, although Sherman himself probably would have considered Napoléon to have been the great innovator in this realm, and Genghis Khan had been no slouch either. Writing a decade after the war, Sherman concluded about his intentions during the last year of his campaigning, "My aim then was, to whip the rebels, to humble their pride, to follow them to their inmost recesses, and make them fear and dread us."[28]

On the long march through the Confederate heartland, although he sponsored the burning of the southern food supply, the theft and killing of draft animals, and the burning of barns, fields, and fences, Sherman also prohibited the rape of southern women, the killing of civilians, and, on the whole, the burning of occupied rural houses and of towns. Unlike the combatants on both sides of the guerrilla war, Sherman never intended in actual practice, nor would he permit, a level of destructive war that would erase the line between civilian and military enemies. He intended to induce terror and to make psychological war, but unlike guerrillas, he did not even dream of genocide against southern whites, whom he viewed as errant fellow-civilians to be defeated as efficiently as possible in war in order to welcome them back, chastised and redeemed, into the bosom of the Union family. In his attack on southern hearts, Sherman stopped well short of total warfare. He certainly had the military means to make total war—overwhelming force and no viable opposing army—which allowed his torch-bearers to fan out over a broad swath of land, and he perhaps had sufficient personal anger and self-righteousness to wage a total war if he had really wanted one, but he held himself and his men back because of the shared cultural value system which would not permit the slaughter of white American civilians.

As was generally true in his culture, as the Sand Creek massacre of 1864 had demonstrated once again, Sherman too did not consider Indians to be part of the true American family—these were not errant kin, as were white southerners, but alien savages. Toward Indians, he could at least countenance a war of extermination, the killing of all civilian men, women, and children. In mid-nineteenth-century America, paternalistic, protective, and even romantic images of Indians vied with the picture of nomadic heathens fit to be slaughtered. Sharing these ambiguities, Sherman rarely expressed completely genocidal feelings toward Indians. However, especially writing in private to old Civil War comrades, when he was in charge of the war against the Plains Indians, which accompanied the building of the transcontinental railroad after the Civil War, Sherman not only used a language approaching genocide, but he seemed to predict the death not merely of Indians but of the Indian culture and people in a manner in which he had never conceptualized white Georgians and Carolinians even when he was in the midst of attacking them.

Exasperated by the guerrilla tactics of the childlike red devils, Sherman wrote from his St. Louis headquarters to Ulysses S. Grant, the Army commander in Washington in 1867, "In time we must take these wild Indians in hand and give them a devil of a trashing. They deserve it now, but they are so scattered and so mixed up that even if we were prepared, we would hardly know which way to strike." However exasperated he was, Sherman had only a tiny army to cover a huge area of the West, and thus only limited means to act out his urgent feelings (unlike his far stronger military situation in 1864–65 in the South). Even in a cooler mood, writing again to Grant in 1868, Sherman viewed Indians as a separate and inferior race to be "removed." Whether or not ultimate justice was on the side of the white race, History was, Sherman believed, and he also believed himself to be Destiny's Agent. "I have no doubt our people have committed grievous wrong to the Indians and I wish we could punish them but it is impracticable," Sherman wrote to Grant in 1868, in one of his more complex formulations of the "Indian problem." "Both races cannot use this country in common and one or the other must withdraw. We cannot withdraw without checking the natural progress of Civilization. The only course is for us to destroy the hostile, and to segregate the peaceful and maintain them." To this point in his analysis, Sherman saw himself as a compromising father, mediating between furious white settlers and hostile Indians, seeking to protect the good Indians while punishing only the bad. Sherman, however, went on. Although he would not commend or sponsor the slaughter of tame bands, as had been the case at Sand Creek, Sherman wrote to Grant, "I would not hesitate to approach the extermination of a camp . . . from which they send out their thieving and murderous parties to kill and steal." Selecting only the bad Indian women and children for death might well merge, Sherman considered, into a more wholesale slaughter. If Indians did not distinguish between white soldiers and white settlers, Sherman wrote to Grant, "We in our turn cannot discriminate among the Indians—all look alike and to get the rascals, we are forced to include all."[29]

If a touch of ambivalence remained here while he was at his calmest, if generally he did not seek to enact the exterminationist values he shared with almost all white settlers in the West, Sherman often could override his human inhibitions when he considered the Indians that he was fighting on the Plains, in a manner impermissible to him when he had attacked white southerners. Indeed, at his most furious, Sherman could lift his verbal censorship. On December 28, 1866, after Captain William J. Fetterman and eighty-one of his men were killed near Fort Phil Kearney, in what is now northern Wyoming, Sherman wrote to Grant, "We must act with vindictive earnestness against the Sioux, even to their extermination, men, women, and children. Nothing else will reach the root of this case."[30]

What had been unthinkable to the erstwhile father leading the honor-bound family, the incorporation of even errant children who were to be punished before they were redeemed, was quite thinkable toward others outside one's concept of shared peoplehood. Thresholds of violence varied in both varieties of warfare, of course. White warrior brother shot and mutilated white brother in Missouri, and this was not the case when two regular armies faced off in the larger Civil War. But in neither the guerrilla nor the regular war sector was sister, mother, wife, or daughter raped or murdered as a general rule. Not only guerrillas but regular soldiers too could rape and slaughter Indian women and children, and Confederates would shoot disarmed black soldiers, which they would not allow themselves to do to members of the white culture, even enemy ones. Sherman, who consciously fought with brutality against Georgia to make reunification and peace, warred against the Sioux to drive them off the land, and if necessary to exterminate them. On the great stage of the Civil War, even Sherman, the most articulate mass terrorist, held back at the gate of total war against civilians. Only toward the Indians did he reach toward this level of destructiveness of a whole people.

In the guerrilla war and in the war against the Indians, one can catch glimpses of what might be called the great chain of cultural antibeing. In the Anglo-American experience of this chain, one might start with the English treatment of the "barbarian," "heathen," Irish, who were to be treated as the English refrained from treating one another. English martial debasement and destruction of the Irish had a long lineage, dating back to at least the twelfth century, when, John Gillingham has argued, the developing rules of chivalric combat, including exchange of prisoners rather than their enslavement or slaughter, simply were not applied by the English to the Irish, who were not conceptualized as fellow humans with whom to bargain equally but as aboriginal savages to be killed when they were in the way.[31]

England's more direct moral predecessor to Sherman, one to whom he was compared frequently after the war, would be Oliver Cromwell, a morally upright and generally humane man, who told his officers when he assumed command in Ireland in 1649, "I have often had these thoughts within myself which perhaps may be carnal and foolish: I had rather be overrun by a Cavalierish interest than a Scotch interest, I had rather be overrun by a Scotch interest than an Irish interest, and I think that of all this is the most dangerous. . . . If they shall be able to carry on their work they will make this the most miserable people in the earth, for all the world knows their barbarism." Cromwell proceeded to storm Drogheda, slaughtering its 2,800 inhabitants, and then Wexford, killing 1,500. Far from showing remorse for these massacres, after Drogheda he wrote "I am persuaded that this is a righteous judgment of God upon those barbarous wretches, who had imbrued their hands in so much innocent blood, and that it will tend to prevent the effusion of blood for the future; which are the satisfactory grounds of such actions, which otherwise cannot but work remorse and regret." After Wexford, Cromwell deepened rather than reversed his blooded certainty; he then wrote that he had been God's minister, doing justice to His enemies. "God, by an unexpected providence, in His righteous justice brought a just judgment upon them, causing them to become a prey to the soldiers who in their piracies had made preys of so many families, and with their bloods to answer the cruelties which they had exercised upon the lives of divers poor Protestants."[32]

The following year, Cromwell warred against the Scots, who were to him not Papist savages to be slaughtered but errant Protestants who were to be chastised and then welcomed back into the English family: They were "one's own," Cromwell proclaimed. And within England, Cromwell and the Royalists usually tried to limit collateral damage to civilians: Barbara Donagan has argued that for reasons both of "utility and professional honor," they shared "a kind of contractual etiquette of belligerence."[33]

It has been argued that what the English learned about the aboriginal Irish they then applied to the Indians of America.[34] When they reached for an analogy to analyze what was to their sensibilities barbaric behavior among the Indians, New England Puritans often alighted on the Irish parallel. Observing native funeral customs, including face painting with lead and soot, William Wood noted that the ceremonies were accompanied with "Irish-like howlings." Roger Williams, that most benevolent of New Englanders, argued against the enslavement of Indians who had surrendered, lest they be encouraged to remain enemies "or turn wild Irish themselves."[35] Such a melding of cultural categories among seventeenth-century English settlers in America does lead us toward Sherman, whose attitude about the Indians so resembled those of Cromwell concerning the Irish—set, as both men were, in the context of cultures that would prescribe treating the aliens as Others, as they were at Sand Creek and Drogheda, Wexford, and Fort Pillow.

In their guerrilla conflict, American warriors had approached the destruction of all possible enemies, civilian and soldier alike—the nihilist desire—but, because of their cultural values, however perversely reworked, they had held back from plunging all the way into the abyss. Their attitudes and behavior shifted significantly when they warred against enemies of other races. In this, they resembled seventeenth-century European soldiers and those of our century, who often war against Others as they would not against those whom they consider as their own. Attention to levels of destructiveness of civilians during wars reveals a great deal about the meanings of human conflict obscured by modernization theory. Argument by linear development toward the *modern* or the *total* in war is a kind of teleological trap that obscures more than it reveals about warfare as a widespread and varied cultural institution. Instead of assuming that everything leads to now, by examining the throw of the cultural net, with differing levels of destruction applied to one's own than to the Others, one can begin to understand not a false and foreshortened progression but a long and jagged record, one that reflects concrete cultural circumstances, not abstract chronological imperatives.

THE ACTIONS AND LANGUAGE of Oliver Cromwell and William T. Sherman, both vivid writers and ruthless warriors, drove home my argument about the cast of the cultural net determining the level of violence applied against enemy civilian as well as military populations during wars. Cromwell rank ordered his degree of fear and loathing for the populations he was fighting: English Royalists were not as bad as Scots, who were in turn not as bad as the Irish, those inhuman, Papist, "barbarous wretches," deserving to be slaughtered, armed men and civilians, women and children included. When feeling utterly provoked, as had Cromwell, Sherman explicitly countenanced fighting with "vindictive earnestness" against the Sioux, spelling out that he meant genocide. Even when he thundered against Confederates in his most extreme rants, Sherman never articulated a thirst for extermination, nor did he depopulate large swaths of the enemy South through which he marched, in an ethnic cleansing of the sort the Americans enacted when creating the reservation system. Those markers of war against enemy civilians—my measure of the totality of war—Cromwell applied to the Irish and Sherman to the Indians. These were threatening groups—racial inferiors, subhuman Others—fundamentally unlike one's own.

Licensed destruction of utter aliens is a common attitude leading to similar behaviors in many times and places. The specific identity of the Other deserving annihilation is flexible, deriving from socially constructed norms that differ from culture to culture. During the Thirty Years' War and many other conflicts, nationality, ethnicity, and class have been the grounds on which Otherness was constructed. In the United States, it's not ethnicity or class but race that's the great divider. But these categories can shift according to immediate needs. One hundred years after Cromwell, another English army would take genocidal war to the Highland Scots, defining them just as Cromwell had balked at doing in his day when he smeared and assaulted the barbarian Irish but went easier on the Scots.

Embedded in my argument was the belief that when it became a race war—Confederates against African American Union soldiers—the Civil War approached exterminationism in a way that it did not when it was a fight between two sorts of white Americans. However, in guerrilla warfare white men could exterminate one another when they had the power to do so, although women and children were generally spared. This element of restraint from total slaughter demonstrated a certain fluidity of defining that dehumanized Other when other white people were targeted. Such relative forbearance further demonstrated that race was the key difference in American cultural traditions, one that provided the clear ideological grounds necessary for fighters to license themselves to approach total destruction.

Beyond and beneath my explicit argument lay long-term reactions to what I had learned about the belief structure of American soldiers on the ground in Viet Nam, where civilian men, women, and children—often derogatorily referred to as "gooks"—were the Other fit for annihilation. We have seen this phenomenon in other American colonial wars, including the protracted war against the Indians, the Philippine-American War at the turn of the twentieth century (which I describe in the final chapter of *In the Name of God and Country*), and in much of the Iraq conflict and the War on Terror.

If Americans should not presume that they are morally better than other nations, neither should Americans breast-beat that they are worse than anyone else, in a kind of reverse exceptionalism. All colonizing powers behave in a similarly brutal manner. At the time I was writing, the Serbians were on a rampage, defining Muslim Bosnians—who were linguistically and physically indistinguishable from themselves—as the Other, deserving ethnic cleansing and systemic slaughter. And of course the Germans had perfected this form of genocide against a category of civilians defined as subhuman, threatening, and pestilential. Nazis bureaucratized genocide in a way that can be called modern, but it is uncertain whether they achieved much higher levels of slaughter than have other peoples using more inefficient means. So widespread has been such organized action over the entire run of human existence that discussing total war as a product of modernization to my mind misses its deep repetitiveness.

Several of the conference attendees focused on my almost throwaway line that the tendency toward indiscriminate slaughter, the love affair with nihilism, is "present in all wars (and perhaps in the human breast)." This highly qualified suggestion about which I have never been able to draw a firm conclusion, could be taken either psychologically—as the death wish or the compulsion to destroy—or theologically, as original sin. It was my impression that most of the historians who emphasized this idea were committed Christians. Over the years as well as at this conference—and despite the obvious fact that I am essentially and openly irreligious—I have found that my best discussions about moral structure and moral disintegration have occurred with religious people of whatever persuasion, while secular historians, who make up the majority in the profession, rarely engage in such questioning or regard it as especially significant.

When considering moral disintegration and perverse reintegration among warriors and the civilians they affected, I have been helped by the work of the World War II veteran and philosopher Glenn Grey, a number of psychiatrists who dealt with the psychic wounds of returning Vietnam veterans who had committed atrocities, and the books of Robert Jay Lifton, a tough-minded ego psychologist. But when I was attempting to get past repulsion to try to comprehend extreme but common behaviors such as mutilation and torture as I worked on *Inside War*, I felt the need to go beyond books and to talk with people who had been there. While spending the years 1982 and 1983 at the Shelby Cullom Davis Center for Historical Studies at Princeton University, where this project took shape, I had long conversations with the political scientist Walter Murphy, a Marine lieutenant in Korea, and the historian Richard Challaner, a combat veteran of the European theater of World War II. In particular I recall one four-hour lunch with Murphy at a diner on the edge of town. I would ask him about something horrendous I had found in the archives, and he would rub his hand across his forehead and draw out a deeply painful memory of the behavior of the soldiers in his platoon that was similar to the stories I knew from the Civil War. Then I would apologize for causing him pain, but he would urge me to continue; as a political scientist he knew he was my "native informant," and that I was not asking questions gratuitously or sensationalistically. In the years since, combat veterans have often opened up to me whether in person after a lecture or via e-mail. They all know that they had lived in fear and loathing of the enemy, but also in loving brotherhood with their fellow soldiers, in an alternative culture that both grew out of their previous and subsequent civilian culture and violently denied its peaceful everyday norms.

In 1989, right before the slaughter at Tiananmen Square, I gave a seminar at the history department of Sichuan University in Chengdu, where I had another powerful experience that helped me to sort out some of the meanings of warriors living on the nihilist edge. After I discussed the political violence of guerrilla warfare in Missouri, with the help of a brilliant translator, I asked the Chinese faculty and graduate students how my findings correlated with their experiences of the Cultural Revolution. Perhaps I intuited what might ensue, but I cannot recall how conscious I was about the potential implications of the question. In the event, I learned that the younger men sitting around the table had been Red Guards, who had persecuted many of the older professors in their department sharing that seminar room. Clearly they had all learned to live and work together after the Cultural Revolution ended, and intellectual life was reconstructed. But it was not clear to me that they ever had discussed what had happened, certainly not in a public forum. I told them that I feared I had been unintentionally callous in bringing up this subject, but they reassured me that they understood that I was asking a question of concern for fellow professional historians and they wanted to go on.

Over the next three hours, with anguished openness, they tried to reconstruct what had happened. The chief focus of the memories of the younger men was on peer pressure to conform to a policy of committing violence against their elders, even people they admired and loved. They did not deny these acts; neither did they describe them in detail. They all agreed that this coercion to participate in personal brutality was almost unaccountable—they felt continued shame, but also the need to distance themselves from their past actions in order to survive personally and to move back into creative community with the people they had attacked. Their victims, the older men in the room, were more reticent, stressing that they had learned to forgive through understanding the powerful ideological impulses behind the Cultural Revolution. One professor said that being forced to live with the peasants was intended to be a great humiliation, but that he liked peasants and had a good time with them while in intellectual exile. None of the victims wanted to discuss specific incidents, although they assured me that much of what I had found in Missouri they had lived through in Sichuan province, some of it by the young hands in their very university department. Perhaps this discussion was cathartic as well as distressing—I certainly hope it was.

During the American Civil War, Francis Lieber, the immigrant German American legal scholar who drafted General Orders #100 guiding the conduct of soldiers when fighting guerrilla war, had learned about the viciousness he wanted to curtail in conversation—that must have been rather similar to those I had with members of the Sichuan University history department —with General Henry Halleck, who had been in command in Missouri early in the war, and with other officers who had experienced such warfare. In this code you can see the irresolvable internal tension between Lieber's continuing ideal of civilized warfare and the realities of fighting guerillas. Civilized warfare of the sort the American army theoretically should practice was based on humanity not tyranny; ideally it was to be conducted not with "cruelty but by the principles of justice, honor, and humanity." On the other hand, guerrillas not fighting with honor, but as "highway robbers or pirates," were to be shot rather than taken prisoners of war. In the deep confusions of guerrilla war, where enemy fighters blended into the civilian population who aided them, who was and who was not the despicable hidden enemy? Because suspicion rather than certainty characterized most counterinsurgent actions, honor and justice always tended to disappear and indiscriminate slaughter always tended to replace it. Lieber placed this contradiction at the center of a code, which meant that the restraints he juxtaposed to his calls for ruthless action almost always disintegrated in the field. General Orders #100 served more as a protective device for those writing military reports than as a guide to action, where the terrors of the moment dictated the most brutal responses.

Perhaps American commanders had a greater need than officials in less democratic societies to present the facade of justice in the reports they published when injustice was the norm in practice. Filing reports invariably led to denial and hypocrisy rather than honest admission about the realities of guerrilla warfare. I took it as my historical task to go beyond the official justifications and obfuscations in order to plumb the nihilist beliefs and actions of soldiers who actually had been engaged in such combat, to try to discern the personal and social reconstruction they needed in order to carry on fighting such fights. After the war, the victorious Union Army would write the history, leaving out their own atrocities and stressing those committed by their Confederate guerrilla opponent, defeated men who had no means to challenge their enemy's version of events.

This was all gloomy territory to attempt to reconstruct. Indeed it took me several years before I could write about mutilation and torture. My initial take was that war is hell and people are shits, and although I continue to believe that proposition, it was an insufficient framework on which to construct a book. Therefore, studying the psychological literature and talking with former soldiers and their victims gave me better framing devices to use in order to develop a deeper understanding of what I was reading. I needed some, but not too much, distance in order to come to grips with the immediacy of the horrors I had found.

While I was writing my book on Missouri, I reached the conclusion that the insides of the war experience are indeed savage, and that the dream of annihilation of the Other is fully human: when shared by men acting in concert it is best defined as social rather than antisocial or asocial behavior. But equally human are the needs to cooperate, to build, to share, to nurture. We have multiple capacities, all of which are human. Original sin is not all there is within us, but that capacity to obliterate is there, just as is "original love."

Although the book and the essay that followed it focused on Missouri and really concerned that conflict, the work was intended inferentially as my book on Vietnam. And it was written to address my perplexity with the experience of political violence and war, and not just in Missouri or the Civil War or even the American experience of war, although certainly at that time and locale in particular.

NOTES

1. I wish to thank Robert H. Wiebe, John Gillingham, and Santa Aloi for their perceptive readings of earlier drafts of this chapter.

2. Johann Jakob Christoffel von Grimmelshausen, *Theatrum European* I (Frankfurt/ Main: Meridan, 1643), 1050, paraphrased in Herbert Langer, *The Thirty Years' War* (Poole, England: Blandford Press, 1980), 105.

3. Geoffrey Parker, *The Thirty Years' War* (London: Routledge & Kegan Paul, 1984), 127. For this passage, Parker cites Ernst L. Sticht, *Markgraf Christian von Brandenburg-Kulmbach und der Dreissigjährige Krieg in Ostfranken, 1618–1635* (Kulmbach, 1965), 164.

4. Harry Kamen, "The Economic and Social Consequences of the Thirty Years' War," *Past and Present* 39 (April 1968): 44–62; Parker, *The Thirty Years' War,* 164.

5. Parker, *The Thirty Years' War,* 208–15. In addition to Parker's macromilitary and political analysis and Langer's cultural history, the best narrative of this war in English remains C. V. Wedgwood, *The Thirty Years' War* (London: J. Cape, 1938). The cold-bloodedness of much of the historiography of the Thirty Years' War is approximated perhaps only by that found in the discussion of the demographic catastrophe in the central valley of Mexico during the first one hundred years after white contact and conquest. The refusal to focus on the "microlevel" sufferings of ordinary people, while examining huge and hugely impersonal demographical "death rates," strikes me as monumentally insensitive. A second early modern conflict filled with dehumanization and slaughter of civilians was the epoch of the French civil wars of religion, on which the most complete analysis is in Denis Crouzet, *Les guerriers de Dieu: La violence en temps des Troubles de Religion, vers 1525–vers 1610,* 2 vols. (Seysell: Champ Vallon, 1990). For a brief summary by Crouzet of his thesis, see his "Violence Catholique et désir de Dieu," *Notre Histoire* (April 1992):

36–40. I am much obliged to Annette Becker for these references. It is one of Russell F. Weigley's themes in *The Age of Battles* (Bloomington: Indiana University Press, 1991) that eighteenth-century military leaders consciously attempted, not always with success, to pull back from the horrors of seventeenth-century warfare, which had gone much too far to suit their minds and stomachs.

6. For a good scholarly analysis of the twentieth-century linguistic creation of the term "total war," argued in the context of the American Civil war depicted as less than a total war, see Mark E. Neely's stimulating essay, "Was the Civil War a Total War?" *Civil War History* 37 (1991): 5–28.

7. These generalizations, and the discussion of guerrilla war that follows are extrapolations from my book, *Inside War: The Guerrilla Conflict in Missouri during the American Civil War* (New York: Oxford University Press, 1989). The notes to that book also provide bibliographical and historiographical context.

8. The best discussions of General Order no. 11 are Charles R. Mink, "General Orders no. 11: The Forced Evacuation of Civilians during the Civil War," *Military Affairs* 34 (December 1970): 132–36, and Ann Davis Niepman, "General Orders no. 11 and Border Warfare during the Civil War," *Missouri Historical Review* 67 (January 1972): 185–200.

9. War Department, General Order no. 100, Washington, D.C., April 24, 1863, *The War of the Rebellion: A Compilation of the Official Records of the Union and the Confederate Army,* ser. 3, vol. 3, (Washington, D.C., 1880–1902), 148–64. This compilation is hereafter cited as *OR.* For Halleck's request to Lieber for an analysis of the legal context in which to consider guerrilla warfare, and Lieber's reply, see Lieber's essay, "Guerrilla Parties Considered with Reference to the Laws and Usages of War," ser. 3, vol. 3, *OR,* 301–9.

10. Major General Samuel R. Curtis to Captain J. C. Kelton, Batesville, May 19, 1862, ser. 1, vol. 13, *OR,* 392; Colonel James H. Ford to O. D. Greene, Independence, July 26, 1864, Two or More Name file 2635, record group 393, Records of U.S. Army Continental Commands, 1821–1920. Dept. of the Missouri, National Archives, Washington, D.C.; George Woltz to His Parents, Springfield, Aug. 11, 1862, Joint Collection, University of Missouri, Western Historical Manuscript Collections—Columbia, State Historical Society of Missouri Collections (hereafter cited as JC); Lieutenant Colonel Bazel F. Lazear to Captain Dyer, Jackson, February 14, 1863, ser. 1, vol. 22, pt. 1, *OR,* 224–25; William C. Long to His Children, Butler, Dec. 23, 1863, William C. Long papers, JC; Captain Thomas Thomas to Captain J. Lovell, Houston, Jan. 11, 1864, ser. 1, vol. 34, pt. 2 *OR,* 57.

11. Major Austin A. King to Brigadier General Clinton B. Fisk, Fayette, Sept. 14, 1864, ser. 1, vol. 41, pt. 3, *OR,* 194; *Missouri Statesman,* Aug. 5, 1864. Concerning scalping, the most sophisticated discussion is James Axtell, *The European and the Indian: Essays in the Ethnohistory of North America* (New York: Oxford University Press, 1981), 16–35.

12. Brigadier General Clinton B. Fisk to Lieutenant Colonel Daniel M. Draper, Macon, Ga., April 18, 1864, ser. 1, vol. 24, pt. 3, *OR,* 216.

13. For a brilliant discussion of the aesthetic of destruction among men in war, see J. Glenn Gray, *The Warriors: Reflection on Men in Battle* (Lincoln: University of Nebraska Press, 1959). For psychological analyses of soldiers who commit atrocities, see William Barry Gault, "Some Remarks on Slaughter," *American Journal of Psychiatry* 128, no. 4 (Oc-

tober 1971): 450–54; William Goldsmith and Constantine Cretekos, "Unhappy Odysseys: Psychiatric Hospitalizations among Vietnam Reporters," *Archives of General Psychiatry* 30 (January 1969): 78–83; Sarah A. Haley, "When the Patient Reports Atrocities: Specific Considerations of the Vietnam Veteran," *Archives of General Psychiatry* (February 1974): 191–96; Joel Yager, "Personal Violence in Infantry Combat," *Archives of General Psychiatry* (February 1975): 257–61. In general, my analysis of the psychological meanings of warfare owes a great deal to the work of Robert J. Lifton. Of his opus, see in particular *The Nazi Doctors: Medical Killing and the Psychology of Genocide* (New York: Basic Books, 1986); *Death in Life: Survivors of Hiroshima,* 2nd ed. (New York: Weidenfeld and Nicolson); *Thought Reform and the Psychology of Totalism: A Study of Brainwashing in China,* 2nd ed. (New York: W. W. Norton, 1961); *Explorations in Psychohistory: The Wellfleet Papers* (New York: Simon and Schuster, 1974); and with Eric Markusen, *The Genocidal Mentality: Nazi Holocaust and Nuclear Threat* (New York: Basic Books, 1990).

14. Fellman, *Inside War,* 3–11.

15. An ambitious book on many of these themes is Bertram Wyatt-Brown, *Southern Honor: Ethics and Behavior in the Old South* (New York: Oxford University Press, 1982). See also Dickson D. Bruce, Jr., *Violence and Culture in the Antebellum South* (Austin: University of Texas Press, 1979), and Edward Ayers, *Vengeance and Justice: Crime and Punishment in the 19th Century American South* (New York: Oxford University Press, 1982).

16. Daniel R. Smith to His Parents, Jefferson City, Aug. 28, 1861, Daniel R. Smith papers, Illinois State Historical Library, Springfield.

17. Edwin F. Noyes to Mr. Stephenson, Camp Benton, Aug. 21, 1861, Nathaniel Wright Family papers, Library of Congress, Washington, D.C.

18. Deposition of Mrs. Mary Hall, Franklin County, May 11, 1865, Letters Received file 2593, Record Group 393, National Archives.

19. Sophia L. Bissell to Her Cousin, Lawrence, September 8, 1863, Sophia L. Bissell letters, Chicago Historical Society.

20. Charles M. Chase to the editor of the Sycamore, Illinois, *True Republican and Sentinel,* Independence, Mo., Aug. 12, 1863, reprinted in *The Kansas Historical Quarterly* 26 (1960): 124.

21. Entry for May 25, 1862, Sardius Smith diary, Illinois State Historical Library.

22. Fellman, *Inside War,* 28, 39–40, 181, 206, 252.

23. Court-Martial of James Johnson, Jefferson City, May 18, 1863, case MM 1021, record group 153, Judge Advocate General—General Court Martial Records, National Archives; Mrs. J. R. Roberts to General James L. Long, Quincy, Illinois, April 7, 1864, Provost-Marshal file, Letters Received file 2786, record group 393, National Archives. On white treatment of blacks, particularly but not exclusively those in the Union Army, see Joseph T. Glatthaar, *Forged in Battle: The Civil War Alliance of Black Settlers and White Officers* (New York: Free Press, 1990).

24. Report of First Lieutenant James D. Cannon, 1st Infantry, New Mexico Volunteers, Fort Lyon, Colorado Territory, Jan. 16, 1865, ser. 1, vol. 41, pt. 1, *OR,* 970–71; Joint Committee on the Conduct of the War, Massacre of the Cheyenne Indians, 28th Congress, 2nd session (Washington, D.C., 1865); Report of the Secretary of War, 29th Congress,

2nd session, Senate Executive Document 26 (Washington, D.C., 1867). Parts of these two official investigations are reprinted in John M. Carroll, ed., *The Sand Creek Massacre: A Documentary History* (New York: Amereon House, 1973). See also Stan Hoig, *The Sand Creek Massacre* (Norman: University of Oklahoma Press, 1961).

25. Albert Castel, "The Fort Pillow Massacre: A Fresh Examination of the Evidence," *Civil War History* 4 (1958): 37–40; John Cimprich and Robert C. Mainford, Jr., "Fort Pillow Revisited: New Evidence about an Old Controversy," *Civil War History* 28 (December 1982): 293–306; James McPherson, *Battle Cry of Freedom* (New York: Oxford University Press, 1988), 748; Glatthaar, *Forged in Battle*, 155–59; and for Poison Springs, ser. 1, vol. 39, pt. 1, *OR*, 554–57. One can only approximate the exact number of blacks who surrendered and were then executed. There were 295 whites and 262 blacks garrisoned at Fort Pillow when Forrest's men attacked. One hundred and twenty-seven whites were killed and 168 taken prisoner. Of the blacks, only fifty-eight were taken prisoner. Assuming, for the purposes of estimation, that approximately the same proportion of blacks as whites (36 percent, or ninety-four men) were killed in battle, 110 were killed after surrendering.

26. Ser. 1, vol. 39, pt. 3, *OR*, 660.

27. William Tecumseh Sherman, *Memoirs* (New York: De Capo, 1983), 2: 126–27.

28. Sherman, *Memoirs*, 2:249.

29. Sherman to Grant, June 11, 1867, May 8, 1868, in John Y. Simon, ed., *The Papers of Ulysses S. Grant* (Carbondale: Southern Illinois University Press, 1967), 18:174–75, 261. Also revealing is Sherman's later correspondence with General Philip H. Sheridan, after Grant became president, Sherman the army commander in Washington, and Sheridan the Indian killer in charge in the West; cf. The Sheridan papers, Library of Congress. Sherman's place for the Indian in his value structure, far from original, was the standard one for nineteenth-century Americans, particularly those in the West. "Frontiersmen" were, after all, physically displacing Indians. Such had been the task of the Ohioans of Sherman's father's generation, and such was central to Sherman's purpose on the Great Plains from after the Civil War until his retirement in 1883. For a telling example of this process as it was carried out by civilian settlers in Illinois, from approximately 1800 to 1850, see John Mack Faragher, *Sugar Creek: Life on the Illinois Prairie* (New Haven, CT: Yale University Press, 1986). New England's first settlers brought exterminationist sentiments with them, folk beliefs that only increased after contact. See Richard Slotkin, *Regeneration through Violence: The Mythology of the American Frontier, 1600–1860* (Middletown, CT: Wesleyan University Press, 1973).

30. Sherman to Grant, Dec. 28, 1866, quoted in Robert G. Athearn, *William Tecumseh Sherman and the Settlement of the West* (Norman: University of Oklahoma Press, 1956), 110. Sherman had to operate within a political arena that included former abolitionists and other Christian activists, including his own wife and brother-in-law, who sought to prevent the killing of the Indians and to promote their salvation through conversion to Christianity and to farming. On all elements of this conflict, see the magisterial two volumes by Francis P. Prucha, *The Great Father* (Lincoln: University of Nebraska Press, 1984). Of course, one might argue from our own perspective that destroying Indian religion and economic forms amounted to genocide by softer means, but the narrower point here is

that Sherman could not have gotten away with actual genocide, given American public opinion, which included what Sherman considered to be stupidly humanitarian "Indian lovers," who, whatever his opinion, he could not entirely dismiss. This context can lead us both to underplay and to exaggerate the possible meanings of Sherman's widely shared if ferocious attitudes.

31. John Gillingham, "The English Invasion of Ireland," in Brendan Bradshaw, Andrew Hadfield, and Willy Maley, eds., *Representing Ireland* (Cambridge: Cambridge University Press, 1992), and "Conquering the Barbarians: War and Chivalry in Twelfth-Century Britain," *Haskins Society Journal* 4 (1993) 67–84.

32. The passages on Ireland are quoted in Charles Firth, *Oliver Cromwell and the Rule of the Puritans in England* (New York: G. P. Putnam's Sons, 1900), 252, 256. Such English attitudes toward the Irish have persisted in England, much as have American prejudices toward Indians and blacks. On nineteenth-century English slurs against the Irish, see two books by Lewis P. Curtis, Jr., *Anglo-Saxons and Celts: A Study of Anti-Irish Prejudice in Victorian England* (Bridgeport, CT: Conference on British Studies at the University of Bridgeport, 1968), and *Apes and Angels: The Irishman in Victorian Caricature* (Washington, D.C.: Smithsonian Books, 1971), a study based on cartoons in the popular press. One high Victorian, the historian Edward A. Freeman, noted of the Anglo-American Others during his first visit to America: "This would be a grand land if only every last Irishman would kill a negro, and be hanged for it." Edward A. Freeman to F. H. Dickinson, New Haven, Dec. 4, 1881, in W. R. W. Stephens, ed., *The Life and Letters of Edward A. Freeman,* 2 vols. (London: MacMillan and Co., 1895), 2:242.

33. Barbara Donagan, "Codes and Conduct in the English Civil War," *Past and Present,* no. 117 (February 1988): 78–79.

34. Winthrop D. Jordan, *White over Black: American Attitudes toward the Negro, 1550– 1812* (Chapel Hill: University of North Carolina Press, 1968), 85–91. Jordan entitles this portion of his study, "The UnEnglish: Scots, Irish, and Indians." Also sensitive to white treatment of Indians as well as of blacks is George M. Fredrickson, *The Black Image in the White Mind: The Debate on Afro-American Character and Destiny, 1817–1914* (New York: Harper Row, 1971). Nicholas P. Canny makes the link between sixteenth-century English attitudes toward the Irish and later English-settler takes on the Indians of the New World in "The Ideology of English Colonization: From Ireland to America," *William and Mary Quarterly,* 3rd ser., 30 (October 1973): 575–98.

35. Both quotations are from Alden T. Vaughan, *New England Frontier: Puritans and Indians* (Boston: Little, Brown, 1965), 42–43, 208. Vaughan points out that Williams nevertheless requested an Indian captive for himself.

4

Alligatormen and Cardsharpers

DEADLY SOUTHWESTERN HUMOR

ONE CRISP FALL DAY IN 1982, I was sitting in my basement office in Dickinson Hall at Princeton University when Tony Grafton, a then-young medievalist, stuck his head in my door and asked, "Do you know any good stories?" I asked in return whether he meant dirty ones or otherwise, but he just repeated the question. For some reason, Mark Twain immediately popped into my mind, and I told Grafton that Twain knew a good yarn or two that I could relate. Grafton then told me that the department was setting up a lecture series on "narrativity," a fancy renaming of a traditional form of history writing then making a comeback in response to the chronologically amorphous quality of much social history. Lawrence Stone, the gifted English historian who was the director of the Shelby Cullom Davis Center for Historical Studies at Princeton, and the Italian academic Carlo Ginsburg, then at the very cutting edge of cultural history, were to be the other lecturers. I decided to take up Grafton's offer to fill out the series.

That was flattering company, and besides, as a visiting fellow at the Davis Center, I had few duties beyond giving one paper and attending the notoriously brutal weekly seminars of the center. My primary task that year was to work on *Inside War*—and I was close to Washington, D.C., and the National Archives, where I spent most of several months doing research in the military records of Missouri. But preparing my lecture provided a welcome diversion. The sources necessary for research, including several obscure nineteenth-century travel books and equally obscure folklore journals, were all at hand at the magnificent Firestone Library that

Portions of this chapter were first published in *Huntington Library Quarterly* 49 (Autumn 1986): 307–23.

housed a huge and underappreciated collection of western Americana donated by grateful alumnus and historian Phillip Ashton Rollins.

It turned out that Jeanne Stone, Lawrence's interesting and welcoming wife, was an exacting seamstress; after hearing about my lecture she kindly suggested sewing me a western riverboatman's shirt for the occasion and found a pattern for it. The blue jeans I already owned, and I added a nice red bandana to the outfit. After my introduction by a bemused and not entirely approving professor Grafton, I strode to the podium and let out an enormous "WHOO-OOP!" followed by the wild keelboatman rap that begins the following paper, rendered in a poor imitation of Missouri dialect that was just good enough to fool this audience. At that "WHOO-OOP!" Marta Petrusewicz, a young Polish historian, then a visiting professor at Princeton, who had been turned around to chat with someone behind her as I was introduced, yelled and jumped up in fright, bruising her thighs on the fixed desks of the lecture hall and whooping in pain. This was a most gratifyingly macabre addition to the reading of my text.

Twain read out loud proved to be beautiful and very, very funny. Warming up the audience by getting them laughing made the brutal mocking of poor people I analyzed in my lecture all the more emotionally charged: I first enticed my listeners into sharing the contempt, and then led them to understand the condescending and downright nasty implications of this genre of humor that they had just been enjoying.

After leaving Princeton, I began to rewrite what had been a very oral presentation into an essay suitable for publication. During the next few years, two or three history and American studies journals turned it down; rather than feeling discouraged, I kept rewriting, thickening the analysis, and condensing an already fairly dense argument. I recall almost losing the sense of lives that had been lived and stories that had been told so intent was I on "working through" the theory and the argument. Rarely have I recrafted an essay to this degree—the "beauty" of composition became my uppermost concern, and I hoped I wasn't subverting the raw power of the stories I was recounting.

During my subsequent sabbatical, in 1984–85, I holed up at the Huntington Library in southern California to write the first draft of *Inside War*. While there, Guilland Sutherland, a young British woman who was editing *The Huntington Library Quarterly*—a mixed literature and history journal of high quality and limited circulation—asked if I had a suitable essay for her, which I did. She proved a skillful editor, helping me to prune several digressions and to focus the essay more clearly. So it saw the light of day only to disappear into the black hole into which so many works published in little magazines fall, or so I assumed, until John Mayfield, a distinguished folklorist, told me at a conference in Richmond Virginia in 2002 that the essay was used quite a lot in his discipline. One never knows, does one?

"Alligatormen and Cardsharpers: Deadly Southwestern Humor"

"Whoo-oop! I'm the old original iron-jawed, brass-mounted, copper-bellied, corpse-maker from the wilds of Arkansaw! Look at me! I'm the man they call Sudden Death and General Desolation! Sired by a hurricane, dam'd by an earthquake, half-brother to the cholera, nearly related to the smallpox on the mother's side! Look at me! I take nineteen alligators and a bar'l of whiskey for breakfast when I'm in robust health, and a bushel of rattlesnakes and a dead body when I'm ailing! . . . Whoo-oop! Stand back and give me room according to my strength! Blood's my natural drink, and the wails of the dying is music to my ear! Cast your eye on me, gentlemen, and lay low and hold your breath, for I'm about to turn myself loose!"[1] Thus sings Bob the keelboatman as reported without moral judgment by Huck Finn. Huck has swum from his cozy raft to eavesdrop on the big keelboat, to find out if he and Jim have drifted south of Cairo, downriver of Jim's chance at freedom. They have. But instead of information, Huck gets keelboatman talk and fighting. The Child of Calamity hollers back at Bob, and finally Little Davy threatens to thrash them both. After a violent and inconclusive grown-up brawl, these oversized boys, Bob and the Child, "shook hands with each other, very solemn, and said they had always respected each other, and was willing to let bygones be bygones." Then as the necessity for a bout of hard work interrupted their normal play "they washed their faces in the river; and just then there was a loud order to stand by for a crossing, and some of them went forward to man the sweeps there, and the rest went aft to handle the after sweeps."

Later, back to normal drift, "they sung 'Jolly Jolly raftsman's the life for me,' with a rousing chorus, and then they got to talking about differences betwixt hogs and their different kinds of habits; and next about women and their different ways; . . . and next about what ought to be done with the Injuns; and next about what a king had to do, and how much he got," and so on. Each subject jostled the next in an unformed, credulous manner, as the men-boys slid on down the river (19).

Bob the keelboatman and the Child of Calamity and Little Davy, sons of the muddy Mississippi, are objects of ridicule for Twain, but though primitive and violent they are not presented as really evil. Perhaps it is this lack of evil which made Twain lift this passage out of the novel *Huckleberry Finn*, where all the grown-ups Huck and Jim meet *are* either evil or tainted by evil men or circumstances, and placed the passage instead in *Life on the Mississippi* (1883), which is a piece of the new journalism rather than a novel. In a sense, *Life on the Mississippi* is Twain's sociology behind Huck's story. Through the sociological structures into which Twain places the keelboatman's tale of innocent violence, one can gain a sense of Twain in his role as a late practitioner of the genre of southwestern humor in which the keelboatman was the main character, the central type. I will discuss this type first through its setting in *Life on the Mississippi*, and then through a variety of earlier stories told by others about him. I wish to highlight this sort of character in the context in which he was perceived and used and attacked. These were stories told by western gentlemen and also by easterners, but they were directed almost always to socially aspiring eastern and midwestern audiences. Such characterization, I would suggest, prepared easterners and their economically and culturally ambitious western colleagues to ridicule, debase, and—in combination with historical circumstances and a powerful belief in cultural evolutionism—even to eliminate a broad underclass of men.

In *Life on the Mississippi*, Twain, the former steamboat pilot, came back West from Hartford in 1882 as a journalist to report on life on the great river, with the central focus on steamboating in its dotage. Twain wrote that steamboating, born in 1812, had reached mighty proportions in thirty years, and thirty years after that was nearly dead. Twain reported that the steamboat had "killed the old-fashioned keelboating by reducing the freight trip to New Orleans to less than a week. The railroads have killed the steamboat passages by dragging six or seven steam-loads of stuff down the river at a time, at an expense so trivial that steamboat competition was out of the question." In this passage Twain wrote as an economic determinist. He was also a cultural evolutionist who believed that new types of persons were created by specific progressive economic forms, and that other old types passed on to the trash-heap of history. Twain might like the chaps passed over by history, but he never questioned that they would die out. They were honorable barbarians, "rough and hardy men; rude, uneducated, brave, suffering terrific hardships with sailor-like stoicism; heavy drinkers, coarse frolickers in moral sties like the Natchez-under-the-hill of that day, heavy fighters, reckless fellows, every one, elephantinely jolly, foul-witted, profane, prodigal of their money, bankrupt at the end of the trip, fond of barbaric finery, prodigious braggarts; yet, in the main, honest, trustworthy, faithful to promises and duty, and often picturesquely magnanimous." After a period of transition, steamboats so increased in efficiency that they absorbed all commerce; and "then keelboating died a permanent death. The keelboatman became a deckhand, or a mate, or a pilot on the steamer" (15–16). Thus passed the age fit for the primitive rebel. Elsewhere in *Life on the Mississippi* Twain stressed that the steamboat pilots were scientific, quite educated, and cerebral men displacing the purely physical keelboatmen. Now in 1882, pilots in turn had been displaced by railroadmen whom Twain does not describe in *Life on the Mississippi*. The forces displacing steamboatmen, who had earlier displaced keelboatmen, were modern, mechanical, faceless, nonhuman.

As was always the case for him, Twain was deeply ambivalent about this march of progress. He did like the riverboatmen and regretted their passing. He had been a lordly steamboat pilot, riding high above the river in his wheelhouse, and he continued to admire the pilots' now-disused acumen and nobility, but he surely did appreciate the speed and convenience of railroad traffic. He was always part Huck Finn, but he was also a would-be captain of industry, pouring his fortune into an invention that would render his craft of writing mechanical. He was a one-man encapsulation of the tensions within nineteenth-century American culture as it experienced industrialization. By 1882, he was still the boy from

Hannibal, but he was now living in the big house in Hartford, traveling back to the boyhood home he had long since fled, to gather new tales to add to his old store to take back East, write up, and sell.

Twain tells us, writing in 1883, that he had only left the steamboat pilot's life because the Civil War had forced him out of Missouri (a point to which I will return at the end of this paper). He describes his subsequent career this way: "I had to seek another livelihood. So I became a silver-miner in Nevada; next a gold-miner in California; next a reporter in San Francisco; next a special correspondent in the Sandwich Islands; next a roving correspondent in Europe and the East; next an instructional torch-bearer on the lecture platform; and finally, I became a scribbler of books, and an immovable fixture among the other rocks of New England" (134). His wandering was not directionless: it had led to a stable, respectable conclusion.

As much as he satirized himself here, one should not discount Twain's real pleasure in his progress. He certainly believed he had changed, evolved with the times—he had stormed the fabled East and won fame and fortune telling his own stories of a disappearing West he had forsaken. His mouth was full of pride at the same time it was full of ashes. He loved and he also hated the modern machines and the new industrial man, and he rejected as workplace and living place the villages and the river of nostalgic memory. Twain's keelboatmen were clearly as atavistic to him as they were lovable. They were throwbacks, types from a primitive stage of river culture; they were always nearly violent when not actually being so, though they did have a sly and clever side as well. Twain was writing about them for a more culturally "advanced" audience. As types, they gave his readers a kind of psychological safety-valve: here were almost safely distant folks who behaved with intense, innocent pleasure, and who were also punished for doing so. These were folks upon whom one could project one's own almost safely bottled-up antipathies to an industrial culture already ossifying into nearly European classes and consequent oppressions, while also celebrating one's superiority over men who hadn't even learned the rules against which one was chafing. Twain, both oppressed and oppressor, bore a large personal burden of ambivalence which he shared with his readers—his partial displacements in his writing paid him well while they deepened his sense of contradiction, self-loathing, and growing misanthropy, all of which shot through his laughter.

Whatever the complex sources of his bitterness, Twain had chosen the East. He, the American writer with the best ear ever for southwestern dialect, was affronted when educated westerners lapsed into it in his hearing, or worse, when they accepted dialect as natural language. "I heard a Westerner who would be accounted a highly educated man in any country, say 'Never mind, it *don't make no difference,* anyway.' A life-long resident who was present heard it, but it made no impression upon her. She was able to recall the fact afterward, when reminded of it; but she confessed that the words had not grated upon her ear at the time—a confession which suggests that if educated people can hear such blasphemous grammar, from such a source, and be unconscious of the deed, the crime must be tolerably common—so common that the general ear has become dulled by familiarity with it, and is no longer . . . sensitive to such affronts" (159, emphasis in the original). I read this passage as more straight than satirical. Twain may have loved such talk but he wished to impose grammatical propriety on proper folks—a victory for Miss Watson after all. Certainly, though he bragged in *Huckleberry Finn* of being master of at least seven western dialects, here he wished to make it clear that he both knew and respected standard English. Twain was a spokesman for northeastern linguistic imperialism.

Far more striking than the assumption of merely linguistic superiority in *Life on the Mississippi* is its conclusion: quite opposite to Huck and Jim floating south as the river would take them, Twain is borne *up* the Mississippi against the current, up to the North. "The big towns drop in, thick and fast now; and between stretch processions of thrifty farms, not desolate solitude. Hour by hour, the boat plows deeper and deeper into the great and populous Northwest; and with each successive section of it which is revealed, one's surprise and respect gather emphasis and increase." This was the America of the future, and it worked. It had been built by the new brand of modern Americans. "Such a people and such achievements as theirs, compel homage. This is an independent race who think for themselves, and who are competent to do it, because they are educated and enlightened; they read, they keep abreast of the best and newest thought; they fortify every weak place in their land with a school, a college, a library, and a newspaper; and they live under law. Solicitude for the future of a race like this is not in order" (335).

Let me reverse and rewrite each clause of the last part of that passage, in a manner which, I think, represents Twain's unstated cultural inference: Southwesterners are a dependent race who let others think for them, and who are incompetent to think for themselves because they are uneducated and superstitious; they never read, or read only Sir Walter Scott, which is worse; they ignore all the best and newest thought; they never open new schools, colleges, libraries, or newspapers; and they live outside the law. Solicitude for the future of a race like this is certainly in order. . . . The Northwest was made in the image of the Northeast, and the Southwest ought to follow along. In this implicit rejection of the southwestern style, Twain affirms the outcome of the Civil War and of industrial progress. Knowing his origins, he also knows which direction to travel as a representative modern American, and where the hoped-for point of arrival might be, though here too Twain would become bitterly disappointed.

Furthermore, it is essential to underline Twain's use of the word "race," a definition that he shared with his fellow citizens. In the context of deeply believed-in Progress, races were composites of social types determined by their role in inevitable stages of economic development. Each race was limited to a historically circumscribed set of roles, and when its time passed it was to change into the subsequent race, or disappear, or become an atavistic remnant who could for a time be a quaint source of entertainment for those marching the highway of progress.

Twain wrote within this widespread traditional belief in the cultural evolution of the races and of representative types. *Life on the Mississippi* was a late example of a genre of travel books culturally grounded in the East and Europe, written about the American primitive, who was located in the West. Indeed this primitive was at least as much an Eastern and European expression of the hopes and fears for the Noble Savage as he was a western actuality. In his book on Kentucky, Arthur K. Moore speculates that the human models for the frontier barbarian may have originated unnoticed on the Scots borderland and grown up in the backwoods of Virginia. Moore believes that the ring-tailed roarer came to full form in the first trans-Appalachian settlements in Kentucky immediately after the Revolution. After Indian warfare died down in the early 1790s, these rough men spread from Kentucky through the entire Mississippi River basin, via the keelboat trade. Along this route they became the representative frontier degenerates. To whatever degree the alligator men did or did not exist, we learn of them almost exclusively through literature written after 1810, most often published in the East.[2]

In 1810, in his book *Travels on an Inland Voyage*, published in New York, Christian Schultz presented western primitives to his eastern audience as fully developed alligator men. He overheard two of them, drunkenly bragging at the top of their lungs on the Natchez waterfront. "One said, 'I am a man; I am a horse; I am a team. I can whip any man in *all Kentucky*, by God.' The other replied, 'I am an alligator; half man, half horse; can whip any man *on the Mississippi*, by God.' The first one again, 'I am a man; have the best horse, best dog, best gun, and handsomest wife in all Kentucky, by God.' The other replied, 'I am a Mississippi snapping turtle: have bear claws, alligator's teeth, and the devil's tail; can whip *any man*, by God.' This was too much for the first, and at it they went like two bulls, and continued for half an hour, when the alligator was fairly vanquished by the horse."[3] By 1810, at the latest, in this first-known written description of alligator men, the whole verbal ritual procession is in place. On a question of honor, two keelboaters get drunk, exchange threatening braggadocio, where the idea is to "one up" the other and not to lose one's own cool. Power came from identifying with the most powerful animals in creation, with the alligator as the animal king of the river. Often the shouting match would short-circuit and brawling would ensue, as Huck would later observe, but the ritual was intended to be a limited exchange, to be a sublimation of violence rather than a prelude to it, with cleverness and wit, not fists, as weapons. References were from violent wilderness, not nurturing Nature, but linguistic skill was the preferred medium, for even the roughest alligator man.

These roughneck rituals would change very little throughout the life of the southwestern humor tradition: essentially Twain's raftsmen were Schultz's. Some of this continuity of types is due to the stereotyping formulas inherent in humor; some is also owing to literary marketing mechanisms, as well as to what Hennig Cohen and William B. Dillingham refer to as a "rigid mold" in which southwestern humorists themselves were formed. The lucrative literary marketplace in newspaper, magazine, and book publication was in the East, and for frontier humor there was one critical market, the *New York Spirit of the Times.* Starting in 1831, the editor William T. Porter, a Vermonter who wished to appeal to the sporting gentry of the South and West, solicited southwestern humor, and in addition to providing a first outlet for many new humorists, also put them in touch with New York City publishers. These authors were not poor whites, but physicians, planters, politicians, lawyers, and other men of standing. They were most often devoted Whigs, defensive of their region, but of genteel social proprieties as well. "Seldom has a literary movement or school of writers of any time or place reflected more unanimity in background, temperament, literary products, aims and beliefs," Cohen and Dillingham conclude, a characterization with which all modern scholars of this genre agree.[4]

Editor Porter doubtless had both a sentimentalizing and an inhibiting linguistic impact on his authors, who themselves were searching for gentility. These writers all employed what Kenneth Lynn has called a "self-controlled gentleman" to narrate the stories about the coarse and brutal rip-roarers. Arthur K. Moore has further implied that these authors of social standing were also among the prime land speculators along the frontier, the very men who, through manipulation of courts and legislatures, were in the process of displacing the large class of landless white squatters who were blurred with the smaller group of even more marginal drifters, the alligator men, as the butt of their humor.[5] Indeed the land speculators, who really did win the West and who were deeply resented for it by poor whites, never appear as disreputable literary types, in part of course because they wrote the stories, but also because their goals of clear land title, wealth through accumulation, and security were the unquestioned general goals of an increasingly dominant national middle class. Their satire of the poor whites of their region could have both local and national uses.

These purposes could be continued for most of the nineteenth century through a certain malleability worked into the alligator man image. To a degree, he could be taken off the keelboat and put under steam power. As early as 1826, Timothy Flint described the transition from the pure keelboat type of Schultz's portrait to the steamboat type, the same transition that had fascinated Twain. The "Kentuckian" came to "draw his power" from the steamboat, Flint observed, "and when the warmth of whiskey in his stomach is added to his natural energy, he becomes in succession, horse, alligator, and steamboat."[6] In 1836, in the cabin of his steamboat, the Englishman Joseph Charles Latrobe observed the same sort of chap: "In the manner in which he disposed his person in the cabin, when inactive, upon two or three chairs, basking before the fire, with his nose erect in the air, I thought I detected something of the alligator part of his origin; while in the impetuous manner in which, striding forward with outstretched limbs, he perambulated the cabin or the deck to take exercise, alternately inflating his cheeks, and blowing forth the accumulated air, I could not fail to detect the steam-boat, by which the purity of the race had been recently crossed." Latrobe knew that his readers would relish seeing the American as a cultural primitive. Placing him on a steamboat allowed his modern diffusion, and made even more pointed his culturally atavistic character.[7]

One must stress, however, that the alligator man was often portrayed with an accompanying, second side, as a fellow of stealth as well as of brutality, as a sly fox lurking inside the brutal alligator. Most often this image was presented as a gambler, a cardsharper. In 1844, in a book published in New York, the English comic actor Joseph L. Cowell told of observing a brutal cardsharper who combined wit with violence. Cowell was playing a steamboat game of whist, when he noticed another man who was sitting in, looking over the shoulder of a Virginian gambler, and indicating, by his fingers stretched out on the table, the number of trumps the Virginian held for his confederate across the table to see. "The eagle eye of the Virginian soon detected the villainy, and taking out his [Bowie] knife, . . . began paring his nails with a well-acted indifference, as if entirely absorbed in the game, and laid it quietly on the table. . . . The next hand dealt him one trump and the spy placed his forefinger on the table, which my friend instantly chopped off! 'Hallo! Stranger, what are you about?' shouted the dismembered gentleman. 'You have cut off one of my fingers.' 'I know it,' said old Virginia, coolly; 'and if I had had more trumps, you would have had less fingers.' This was considered an excellent practical joke," Cowell concluded "and we all took a drink together, and I lent the wounded a handkerchief to bind up his hand, which I reminded him last fall at the Gallatin races, that he had forgotten to return."[8] In such stories we can see that the Mississippi riverboat gambler was the younger brother of the alligator man, an expression of the stealth accompanying violence frequently perceived to be resident in the primitive keelboatman.

In many stories, easterners reported being taken in by their own assumption about the stupidity of the keelboatman type. Such easterners knew, the stories go, that those westerners they believed to be ignorant fools in turn used these assumptions to play easterners into traps. The New York journalist William C. Hall reported in 1843 of an evening spent in the dance hall and gambling hells of Natchez-under-the-hill. A very drunk westerner demanded of Hall that he guess the identity of three cards, two with quite visibly bent corners, for $500. Hall could hardly bring himself to take money off such a dim drunk, but while he hesitated, a plainly dressed farmer came along and encouraged him to do so, saying that the drunk was intent on losing his money and that he would hold the stakes. The drunk shuffled, surreptitiously re-bending the corners and Hall of course mis-guessed. "I cast my eyes toward the holder of the stakes—he was in the act of handing them over to the winner, who had suddenly become quite sober, and who, as he pocketed the money, coolly informed me that it was '*all fair*'; and that I had lost my money upon '*My Grandmother's Trick.*'"[9] Hall was the sucker, the easterner caught in his own snobbism. Such stories suggest a self-consciousness by westerners about how easterners had reduced them to a type: they therefore behaved according to type, sometimes using those images for sudden reversals, for flashes of cultural revenge. Alligator men and cardsharpers.

Yet this was defensive cultural counterpunching by the more marginal western frontiersman toward dominant easterners whose greater power stemmed from their control of the levers of economic change and of the press and publishing—the machinery of consciousness. These engines serviced a vision of progress that displayed southwesterners as atavistic pre-progressive types.

This degradation of southwesterners was part of a broader, widely accepted pattern of cultural evolutionism. Let me illustrate further with the table of contents of two travel books about the West published in the East in the 1850s. In *Western Characters or Types of Border Life*, J. L. Mc-

Connell, a popular novelist, wrote ascending chapters on the Indian, the Voyageur, the Pioneer, the Ranger, the Regulator, the Justice of the Peace, the Peddlar, the Schoolmaster, and Schoolmistress, and finally the Politician. I do not know how many of McConnell's readers would have agreed that the politician was the most evolved and civilized type, but the rest of the progression was quite usual.[10] W. P. Strickland, in *Pioneers of the West*, began with explorers, hunters, settlers, and boatmen and ended with the Wisconsin School-ma'am. Each type fitted a stage of economic and social development. Of what he called the "race of boatmen," Strickland concluded, "a milder, gentler race would not have been adapted to the wild, savage region through which they roamed; but they have passed away. These men have fulfilled their mission in the settlement of the West . . . they were useful in their sphere in working out the destiny of the West."[11]

In the course of cultural evolution the usual literary path prescribed for the race of alligator men was downward. Not becoming settled and respectable, they could, most stories went, only degenerate. In his travel book published in 1879, Nathaniel H. Bishop created an interesting parable of the "shanty-boatman's" progress, a kind of corrupt and sex-laden Huck Finn. For his anti-hero, the Mississippi is the River of Cockaigne. For a home, he simply fishes boards and planks from the river. He persuades some wandering Nancy to shack up with him on the all-providing river. "Drifting" will be perfect. "'Nothing to do,' he says, 'but to float with the current, and eat *fresh* pork, and take a hand at eucre.'" The woods are filled with hogs, and he is a crack shot; and farther south "the golden orange shall delight her thirsty soul, while all the sugar-cane she can chew shall be gathered for her." Few of the "fair ones . . . of this class" will refuse such an offer, and so off they drift with the current, the new Adam and Eve. Of course such a temptingly lazy, pleasurable, and sufficient poor man's heaven on earth could not be allowed even in stories. Therefore, reaching New Orleans, the by-now quarrelsome "housekeeper is set adrift" and, continuing her tart's progress, soon is "introduced to city society as Northern Lilly, or Pittsburgh Rose," while her former consort share-crops upriver. His life will remain chaotic, marginal, and worthless, as he will remain "destitute of means," a mere child "of circumstance," one of those "nomads, as restless and unprofitable a class of inhabitants as can be found in all the great West."

In this fantasy, the multitudes of squatters decivilized, merging downward with the more purely antisocial alligator men. This is an anti-family in an anti-relationship with the market economy. There was an element of warning in this picture of what might happen to the very large and unstructured group of poor whites, the better to emphasize to as wide a readership as possible the necessities for the circumscribed and careful life. Bishop drove home this warning by emphasizing that even professors, teachers, and musicians could be found mixed into these rough boat crews, and that "Hundreds of these low fellows will swear to you that the world owes them a living, and that they mean to have it; that they are gentlemen, and therefore cannot work."[12] Gentlemen could be so corrupted by contact with roughnecks as to drop out of proper society, thus making a travesty of all gentlemanly ideals.

The good Bishop emphasized that such downward mobility into indolence almost invariably had its high and almost immediate price, that long before reaching New Orleans on the trip downriver, most keelboats were impaled on unnoticed snags and sunk, abruptly destroying the floating idyll. Generally, insofar as southwestern humor had a *telos*, it was long-term, degenerative drifting, truncated by a graphically depicted violent end. In the climactic fight scene ears and noses were bitten off, eyes gouged out, bowie knives shoved in to the hilt and then twisted. This was the abrupt and nasty conclusion aspiring gentlemen writers deemed appropriate to such low life.

The alternative end for the alligator man, one rarely depicted, would have been to rescue him for social progress, to merge him upward into the propertied, stable, and hence civilized noble yeomanry. John James Audubon told of the rise of one such mythic family. They had left the East of their own free and conscious will because land was too expensive and because they wished their children to become self-sufficient adults. After a long and harsh middle passage, they arrived on the banks of the Mississippi, where they set to work immediately, planting crops, weaving, cutting cord-wood for passing steamboats. Nature provided game and fish, as it had for Bishops' drifters, but Audubon's protagonists also enlarged their fields yearly, and cut and rafted logs to New Orleans, thus mixing their labor with the land. "Who is he of the settlers on the Mississippi that cannot realize some profit?" Audubon asks. "Truly none who is industrious." Hard and persistent work, saving and reinvestment, allowed these squatters to cross up into the vast respectable classes. "Every successive year has increased their savings. They now possess a large stock of horses, cows, and hogs, with abundance of provisions, and domestic comfort of every kind. The daughters have been married to the sons of their neighboring squatters, and have gained sisters to themselves by the marriage of their brothers. The government secures to the family the lands on which, twenty years before, they settled in poverty and sickness. Larger buildings are erected on piles, secure from the inundations; warehouses, stores and workshops increase the importance of the place. The squatters live respected, and in due time die regretted by all who knew them."[13]

Such personal and social regeneration, which one might have thought would have been the goal of western gentleman writers, was in fact opposite to the conclusion of almost all southwestern humor. Audubon was unusual in his optimism and sense of fair play, contrary to the vast majority of humorists who emphasized rather than decreased social distance in their stories, the better to quarantine alien people, thus clarifying for themselves and for their readers the rectitude of proper folks. They sought to tar the much larger squatter class with the animalistic alligator man image, the better to dispossess them.

This degenerate alligator man rather than the hard-working squatter became the archetypal westerner for eastern consumers of these stories. The pervasive literary image ordered the responses of easterners who met westerners face to face. Those easterners who came West to settle indeed brought alligator men and cardsharpers in their minds, and thus wrote back East within the same set of images, if from a slightly different vantage point. Two examples of such preconceived contacts, made during the Civil War in southwestern Missouri, will demonstrate the impact of southwestern humor on the perceptions of middle-class readers. The first is a cartoon drawn by Robert Ormsby Sweeny depicting two well-uniformed Union soldiers questioning, in the road, a pregnant and barefoot young woman who has two naked little children in tow. "'Well old lady are you a Union Woman?' 'No Sir I ain't!' 'Are you a secesh?' 'No Sir, I'm not that neither!' 'Then what the hell are you? I'd like to know.' 'Well, I'd have you'ns know I'm Baptist.'"[14] The second example is from a letter of Colonel of Artillery John Van Deusen, a West Point man, to his father in Hudson, New York, commenting on one reaction to his artillery caisson, which carried a spare wheel in the back. "The ignorance of these people is perfectly tremendous. . . . An old woman came out to look at the battery. 'Well now,' said she, 'I'm an old woman and I thought I had seen enemost everything. My old grandmother used to say that some things were as unnecessary as five wheels to a wagon but I never expected to see a five wheel wagon. I don't want to bother you stranger but will you tell an old woman what that fifth wheel is for?'" Van Deusen concluded, "They had never seen a soldier, a cannon, anything in fact."[15] Art had established categories in which these Union soldiers learned both to deal with and to fend off the poor southwestern whites they met during the war.

In times of crisis, the ridicule and contempt within this form of humor was transformed into a more explicit ideological sword. When push came to shove, as it did in the Civil War and prior to that in "Bloody Kansas" in 1855 and 1856, an antislavery chorus denounced the proslavery Missouri alligator man foe in order to drum up money, arms, and moral support from the East. The foe was not the great plantation owner nor Simon Legree but the sub-human poor white from Missouri, the alligator man, who was made the demonstration case of what evil institutions would do to the small white yeoman of the West. Such a type was now also called a Border Ruffian (referring to the Missouri-Kansas border) and a "Puke" (a term of mysterious but obviously contemptuous origins, perhaps referring to some of the symptoms of malaria, common to settlers of bottom land along the Missouri River). In a propaganda tract published in Boston in 1856, William Phillips described a Puke, *cum* Border Ruffian, a.k.a. alligator man. "Imagine a fellow, tall, slim, but athletic, with yellow complexion, hairy faced, with a dirty flannel shirt, red or blue or green, a pair of commonplace but dark-colored pants, tucked into an uncertain altitude by a leather belt, in which a dirty-handled bowieknife is stuck, rather ostentatiously, an eye slightly whiskey-red, and teeth the color of a walnut. Such is your border ruffian of the lowest type. His body might be a compound of gutta percha, Johnny-cake, and badly-smoked bacon, his spirit, the *refined* part, old bourbon, double-rectified."[16]

Julia Lovejoy, wife of a Vermont Methodist missionary in Kansas, wrote that this type was either fighting or "sucking whiskey," and others chimed in that "They are a queer-looking set, slightly resembling human beings, but more closely allied to wild beasts." Charles Stearns, the Boston *Liberator* correspondent, perhaps the only pacifist abolitionist in all of Kansas, believed he could remain a pacifist while killing Pukes as they were, in his words, "drunken ourang-outans . . . wild beasts. [My] duty [is] to aid in killing them off. When I deal with men made in God's image, I will never shoot them, but these pro-slavery Missourians are demons from the bottomless pit and may be shot with impunity."[17]

Ambiguities disappeared in times of overt conflict. In Bloody Kansas, easterners believed that westerners reverted to type. Put more precisely, easterners placed westerners fully in type during the guerrilla war in Kansas—for them, all that partially sublimated western violence that stemmed from a general cultural regression came out in fighting. If for Twain and earlier writers the alligator men were never fully evil because their violence was politically innocent and was only directed at one another, overt confrontation with them concentrated and distilled the image of their potential for evil when politics was involved and when easterners believed their own fundamental values were immediately threatened. When the crunch came, the lid covering cultural conflict was off. During crisis, the cardsharping alligator man had to be eliminated if Progress were to be served.

I would *not* argue that the stage of physical elimination was an inevitable next step in a historical or rhetorical development. The genocidal conclusion of a Charles Stearns, he of the death-deserving orangutans, was never expressed, probably never overtly believed, in peacetime. The experience of war extended humorous language, justifying actions that would not have been contemplated had war not come in 1856 and again in 1861. The peacetime stereotyping I have described was a more covert and also more sustained means of establishing eastern cultural dominance, a means that would have continued without the Civil War. Thus Stearns's and Lovejoy's objects fit for destruction, those orangutans fighting and sucking whiskey, were in peacetime, as loutish alligator men, already undergoing a prolonged process of delegitimization. The Civil War version probably was not necessary to their displacement. All that said, those long-term images were available to provide some of the basic material for the much more strident attacks needed in times of overt confrontation. In a sense, all that writers had to do to turn southwestern humor into war propaganda was to stop smiling when they said those things.

Thus this genre of stories was deadly in at least two ways: it could be radically heightened in a political emergency to help justify physical elimination of atavistic types; and, in ordinary times, the stories were deadly because they denied the humanity of people different from the dominating and universalizing middle-class, urban, progressive, mainstream spokesmen. The alligator men and their children either had to be converted to decorous middle-class values or else be driven from all power and control of the land. Only a West populated by solid farmers and merchants would serve evolving American capitalism: drifting squatters would never do.

In their literary task middle-class American popular writers employed a vocabulary of "races" and "types" rather than classes, in part to convey the ideal that such races and types automatically dropped away or were forced out or remade themselves during the relentless march of progress. In their own eyes they themselves were not just another race or type but the agents and darlings of progress, which took them right out of their own categories of older types and into what they believed would be a historically inevitable and permanent elect. In this social theory, even though most would refuse ameliorating reeducation, any person potentially could leave an older race voluntarily, could listen to the Wisconsin School-ma'am and harken to Fulton's steam whistle, could join with Mark Twain as he went north toward his new home.

But not all westerners wished to get on the first boat north with Twain. To be fair to Twain, even he was ambivalent about the boat as well as the voyage, and he did deeply wish both to win fame and fortune in Hartford *and* to light out for the Territory. When he became as disillusioned with his adopted eastern values, particularly when they turned jingoistic, as with his natal culture, he was left bitterly isolated. I believe that many ordinary westerners had always shared Twain's divided values: straining for gentility, they were also *in part* alligator men and cardsharpers, enjoying loose language, drinking, and fighting. Let me give one example of an actual barroom brawl during the Civil War, one that demonstrates a certain joy in the anticipation of combat. On 10 October 1863 a very drunken Hendon Hall called out to one Wicks in Wornell's Saloon in Springfield, Missouri, "keep away from me you son of a bitch or I'll blow the top of your head off." When Wicks made no reply, Hall moved menacingly toward him along the bar, shouting "I am a son of a bitch *on wheels,*" drew his pistol and fired. Happily both men were too drunk to hit each other.[18] In our own era Lyndon Johnson's famous comment on Gerald Ford's cerebral capacity should remind us that southwestern humor still lives and is still used from time to time as a weapon by westerners in the hateful yet desired East.

However, westerners did not feel themselves to be *merely* alligator men and they deeply resented an eastern cultural arrogance that they quite understood would render them historical derelicts. In hard times, literary gentlemen were lumped together with the alligator men and squatters they themselves had ridiculed, and it must have been hard for them to be defined without having sufficient means of countering that stereotype which they themselves had done so much to create. This humor had been co-opted and turned against them.

One can find attempted counterattacks if one looks, but not in the eastern media, and not written by lower-class whites. For example, during the crisis over Kansas, some proslavery Missouri newspaper editors responded to the insistence that all southwestern men were whiskey-sucking orangutans, basically by asserting that they in fact were the respectable law and order men and that the Northerners were the hypocritical subversives. "Oh! those long-faced sanctimonious Yankees!" wrote one editor, asking who else would confuse Sharps rifles with the Bible as *moral* weapons. The Yankees were invading devils, wrote another editor under the signature of "Law and Order." "Every man must place a guard around his house to protect his distressed wife and sleeping babies, and dare not pass beyond the rounds of that guard or [he will] be shot down in cold blood." The Yankees were the ones filled with "duplicity, falsehood and hypocracy [sic]"; they really wanted to bed with "stinking negro wenches," to turn "our white men [into] cowards, our black men idols, our women amazons." The Northern invaders sought to turn the world upside down in the name of progress. They, not the Southerners, were the degraded version of the independent white men of modest means.[19]

Class defensiveness linked to regional anger was a common enough expression by those southwestern men whom northerners pummeled ideologically; indeed, this may have been one reason why many non-slave-holding southwestern men sided with the Confederacy against the North during the Civil War. Such ideological battering as they experienced from northeastern pens partially explains the abiding western and southern resentment of Wall Street, the eastern Establishment, *The New York Times*, Harvard, Yale, and England, and it also provides some of the ideological backdrop for populism and other western political outbursts. In addition, one must also always emphasize that today poor whites also live in cities, and that there are vital continuing regional counter-cultures such as those recently portrayed in William Least Heat Moon's *Blue Highways*.[20] Yet western sectionalism continues in opposition to a dominating northeastern cultural domination, the rise of the "sunbelt" notwithstanding. Indeed the depths of resentment stem in part from a fairly clear knowledge on the part of westerners that the power of control over mainstream values remains in someone else's hands.

Let me conclude this discussion of cultural delegitimization with a whimper that grew out of the gigantic bang of the Civil War, Mark Twain's poignant essay, "The Private History of a Campaign That Failed." Here Twain told of becoming a summer soldier in 1861, when he spontaneously joined a southern guerrilla band after, in his words, the Union "invaded our state" of Missouri. Far from the alligator men northerners would have perceived them to be, these were a varied collection of the "young, ignorant, good natured, well-meaning, trivial [boys] full of romance [containing] some pathetic little nickel-plated aristocratic instincts." One boy was "slow and sluggish [but with a] soft heart," another was a "huge, good-natured, flax-headed lubber," and so on. To himself, Twain was simply a silly boy on holiday. After several weeks of frolicsome camping out, one night, hearing that Union forces were advancing on them, six of the fellows hid in a corn crib and fired on an unknown horseman as he approached. As Twain, one of the shooters, looked down on the dying stranger he thought "I had killed a man—a man who had never done me any harm. That was the coldest sensation that ever went through my marrow." Some of the boys stayed on and became guerrilla cut-throats, all too true to Unionist perceptions of them. Others, like Twain, lit out. "We had done our share; had killed one man; exterminated one army." Twain humanized rather than refuted the alligator men—they were after all just a bunch of half-formed boys much like the others."[21] In this tale one can see the killing of Twain's Missouri boyhood home and his banishment, only in part a self-exile, into a lifetime of wandering alienation and such art as he could distill from that boyhood and that long exile. He felt compelled to choose the North because the independent, free-floating, southwestern possibility had been destroyed and could not be put back together. As a remnant Twain saved for all of us that sainted little alligator boy Huck—that much, but not much less or more, could be salvaged from the progress-driven cultural extermination of the race of alligator men and cardsharpers.

Life on the Mississippi had long been one of my favorite books, but until Tony Grafton got me started I had never read it as closely as I read archival documents. I had used novels as texts from time to time, but only for historical illustration. In fact I had chosen history over literature as my field of work, in part, because my undergraduate English professors disliked what they considered my reductionism of the centrality of the text into mere historical evidence. But now I started with Twain and went from there into an interpretation of the ideological meanings of the genre in which Twain wrote, southwestern humor.

Twain was an enormously gifted humorist, a powerful travel writer, a first-rate journalist and sociologist, as well as a writer of scads of bad fiction and several brilliant stories and novels. When, in 1882, he went to the West from Hartford, where he was living big as a famous writer, back to the Old Southwest of his boyhood, Twain was in part doing the research for *Huckleberry Finn*; as I argue in my essay, *Life on the Mississippi* was the sociology behind the story of Huck Finn, the sainted little Alligator Boy. *Life on the Mississippi* was a bit of a hodgepodge, with short stories and rambling conversations embedded in the text, but it was also an enormously witty and thorough study of life back in Twain's natal territory. It was nonfiction composed by a enthusiastic writer looking to discover the core meanings of a society he had rejected and now scorned, even though he still loved it and could never get it out of his system. Like all writers, he made his living alchemizing memory, and humor was the tool he used to deal with the bitter as well as the cherished. Back Home, the Village and the River were the almost timeless past, and Twain was a man eagerly on the cutting edge of the American worship of the new and the constructed, smack dab in the middle of the industrial and urban revolutions brought about by freewheeling capitalism let loose on an enormous and fabulously endowed national landscape.

Twain's central theme in *Huckleberry Finn,* as in *Life on the Missis-sippi,* was cultural displacement. His most powerful characters, from lovely Huck to brutally repellent Pap, were throwbacks—socially atavis-tic personages—remnants of a simpler and untutored bygone era. Despite Twain's enormous sympathy for such figures and his ambivalence about the modern middle class who bought his books—and the society in which he and they were living—Twain was unavoidably connected through his writing genre to a process that I characterized as "cultural delegitimization." As noted in the article, in the Victorian ideology of his day, squatting would never do and drifting was impermissible—solid, sober, dependable economically disciplined citizens were needed to de-velop the country in a "progressive" capitalist fashion.

"Going native" always had been a forbidden temptation. Edmund P. Morgan, in the opening chapters of his magnificent 1975 study of the colonization of Virginia, *American Slavery, American Freedom,* had deeply impressed me with his analysis of how the Indians who preceded the set-tlers managed to live rich, full lives with very little labor and, of course, without Christianity. Virginia's first colonial leaders had had to work hard to smash that alternative, particularly for the indentured quasi-slaves they imported from the bottom of the social order in England, who were tempted to light out for the territory, out of drudgery and into the laid-back Indian way of life. Christian faith tied to economic discipline had been the hallmark of European settlement along the frontier ever since. If uncontrolled, going West might well have led to degeneration—the al-ligator men and cardsharpers the southwestern humorists depicted were the main nineteenth-century stereotypes of this alluring and forbidden alternative cultural possibility, this potentially poisonous fruit.

The more I read in this genre, the more I came to believe that these writers were fighting an ideological class war. During the 1970s, instructed primarily by the influential work of Eugene Genovese and David Brion Davis in American history, and E. P. Thompson and the History Workshop circle in British history, I, like so many other historians, was persuaded that ideological conquest—cultural hegemony—was every bit as important as material domination in the rise of the modern capitalist system. Our sympathy lay with the underdogs, who, as Thompson wrote so memorably, one had to rescue from the enormous condescension of history.

And yet this essay was not really a part of the "history written from the bottom up" approach that characterized most such work, scholarship that was central to my concerns about ordinary people trapped inside war. Rather it was focused on the top-down means by which the captains of culture, in this instance the writers of this genre of humor, delegitimized the undisciplined class of easy livers through their literary production. The key text for describing this process was Antonio Gramsci's *Prison Notebooks*. Gramsci, a sophisticated Italian Communist, had avoided the self-destruction of subordinating himself to Communist Party orthodoxy, rather ironically, when he had been removed from an active role in the party as a result of his jailing by the Mussolini regime for a very long time. Gramsci moved beyond crude and conventional Marxist materialist determinism, arguing that beyond control of the instruments of economic and physical power, the other mode of social domination was cultural—those who seized the heights of "natural" leadership brought a people under their control by deeper and more voluntary means than economic subordination reinforced by sheer force. Gramsci went on to contend that a revolutionary leadership would have to create a counter culture so attractive that the masses of citizens would choose it over the prior regime. While this viewpoint was persuasive to many on the New Left when times appeared to be changing in their favor, by the late 1970s the perspective remained most useful, for me at least, as a means of describing the rapidly increasing domination of the American populace during the nineteenth century by a certain set of values that came to appear universal and unquestionable. That was the core meaning of the building of "cultural hegemony," originally Gramsci's phrase. What later appeared as inevitable was achieved through politically charged creations, including literary ones.

If successive "races" existed on an inflexible social ladder heading toward universal middle-class social values, mocking the "earlier races" as ignorant throwbacks was a powerful cultural battleaxe. "Premodern" meant subhuman. Doing research for an essay published in 1979, I had rediscovered the nickname "Pukes"—given to Missourians in the early nineteenth century—a label much like Michigan "Wolverines" and Wisconsin "Badgers," which were derived from traditional humor. Filthy infantilism as the central quality of strangers you were about to greet, and with whom you were going to compete for land, wealth, and social leadership, certainly seemed an efficient linguistic weapon with which to dehumanize and assault the apparently precivilized men of the Old Southwest. Writers from the East happily used the epithet. These cultural weapons were also easily converted into powerful cultural artillery to be used during the Civil War to shred the humanity of the southern enemy, the better to slaughter him in what proved to be the most lawless theater of guerrilla warfare.

As I noted in the little subessay in note two, I believed that the alligator man/cardsharper was primarily the cultural invention of a specific set of writers. This literature was prescriptive rather than descriptive. After I had completed this paper, Elliott Gorn, the historian of early prizefighting, wrote a celebrated article, replete with sensational and ugly illustrations from nineteenth-century journals, called "'Gouge and Bite, Pull Hair and Scratch': The Social Significance of Fighting in the Southern Backcountry" in which he argued that such extreme fighting was a general phenomenon. Surely it occurred, I agree with Gorn, but how frequently one cannot know; still the real horror derived less from the fights themselves than from the retelling (and embellishment) of stories about such repellent people and events. Writers and publishers interpreted and amplified western violence with their own social and personal needs when they depicted wild westerners for their titillated middle-class readers. The emblematic and literary meanings rather than the literal truths of the violence underpinning southwestern humor made this writing a formidable weapon in the struggle for social hegemony, to whatever degree the brutal fighting Gorn illustrated occurred.

Attempting to analyze the alligator men as actual social actors by leaving out their literary creation struck me as an unintended return to the enormous condescension of middle-class certainties. Before I wrote my lecture, I had had a similar reaction to Eric Hobsbawm's Marxist accounts of nineteenth-century anarchism, *Primitive Rebels* (1959) and *Bandits* (1965). For me, a certain literalness, and the prominent use of the word "primitive," denoted much of the problem with Hobsbawm's elitist approach.

Looking back now, I wonder if my approach was entirely free of my own form of condescension. When one clever Californian friend read the article, he told me that he met lots of cardsharping alligator men at the Santa Anita race track, and I can only guess how much they continue to live on, now derided as country-music loving, hard-drinking rednecks, or, if religious converts, as overly emotional and anti-intellectual Evangelical Christians. Perhaps American cultural hegemony really is divided into blue and red strands; my assumption of a total cultural victory over people derided as primitives was certainly premature and also both unfair and inaccurate. What is the Tea Party if not the recrudescence of alligatorman revenge?

Along these lines my allusion to Lyndon B. Johnson has perhaps been lost for younger readers. In private, the complex and sophisticated Johnson also could be a foul-mouthed southwestern humorist of considerable accomplishment, although his best stuff never made it to print. What he actually said about Gerald Ford, then the Republican Speaker of the House, with whom he worked in a bipartisan way, remains unclear, but it was probably, "Jerry Ford is so dum' that he cain't fart and chew gum at the same time."

My doubts about the universality of one form of cultural domination have caused me to back away somewhat from the Gramscian clarity of this argument. Different people continue to make different sense out of their own lives, whatever majority values may seem to dictate. And what might constitute majority values is highly disputed. And yet, when it comes time to make wars abroad or against internal dissidents— rather frequent occurrences in the modern United States—stereotypes are hauled out to discredit and dehumanize the enemy Other. Liberal societies have many cultural mechanisms to enforce cultural and ideological conformity. The argument from hegemony makes most sense as a description of times when alternative political values become threatening enough to attract widespread denunciation. There is latitude for cultural difference in the United States, but not endless latitude. Under the right circumstances, a wide range of behaviors and beliefs can be considered politically subversive, and so it is not clear when the dragnet reinforcing conformity will descend. Historians should be aware of the many mechanisms of cultural and political domination, and they should always resist signing up with apparently universal social values, that is to say, with patriotism.

I believe that Mark Twain knew all this, and that he realized that he was participating in a culture war about which he himself was deeply torn. As a young man faced with fighting in the Civil War (on the southern side as a Missouri guerrilla), he had lit out west for the territory. Later on, he lit out east for Hartford, and when that soured, he lit out further east for Europe, returning as a deeply alienated, aging man. All this flight was, in some respects at least, a form of drifting; Twain was an alligator man and cardsharper himself after all, as well as a captain of mainstream culture. He invented a persona imbued with highly comic and ironic detachment to try to manage great internal divisions that he never could overcome or even subdue.

Twain became the master of black comedy, which is the best literary means of coping with a society that masks so much discrimination and political violence with seemingly innocent abstractions about freedom, equality, and justice. In the realms of managing ambiguity and laughing in the dark, Twain remains my most profound inspiration.

NOTES

I would like to thank the Shelby Cullom Davis Center at Princeton University and its director, Lawrence Stone, for a visiting fellowship that allowed me to write an earlier version of this essay, and Tony Grafton for asking me if I knew any good stories.

1. Mark Twain, *Life on the Mississippi* (Boston: James R. Osgood and Co.,), 18.

2. Arthur K. Moore, *The Frontier Mind: A Cultural Analysis of the Kentucky Frontiersman* (New York: McGraw-Hill, 1963), 111, 114. On the English origin and frontier translation of backwoods as well as genteel notions of maleness, see the stimulating book by Bertram Wyatt-Brown, *Southern Honor: Ethics and Behavior in the Old South* (New York: Oxford University Press, 1982). In his essay, "'Gouge and Bite, Pull Hair and Scratch': The Social Significance of Fighting in the Southern Backcountry," *American Historical Review* 90

(February 1985): 18–43, Elliot J. Gorn argues that this violence was a real form of behavior for poor whites. Gorn is careless about the number and social context, as well as the geographical and temporal setting of his characters, leaving the impression that most poor whites in the South behaved like this most of the time. He also pays little attention to the social origins and intentions of the compilers of the tales. I would not deny that there were "in fact" some such brawlers, but would stress that they had far greater social meaning as characters in a middle-class morality tale than "in fact." A similar debate occurred some time ago over the "reality" of "social bandits." See E. J. Hobsbawm, *Primitive Rebels* (Manchester: Manchester University Press, 1959), and his *Bandits* (London: Delacorte, 1969), and Anton Blok, "The Peasant and the Brigand: Social Banditry Reconsidered," *Comparative Studies in Society and History*, 14 (September 1972): 494–503. I tend to prefer Blok's argument that the limited and contradictory material reality of the bad man was less significant than his much more widespread psychological reality. I would call this the "emblematic meaning" of the outlaw, although in this essay I stress on the whole his genteel, literary connotations rather than his meanings among the plain folk of the West.

3. Christian Schultz, Jr., *Travels on an Inland Voyage* (New York, 1810), reprinted in John Francis McDermott, *Before Mark Twain: A Sampler of Old, Old Times on the Mississippi* (Carbondale: Southern Illinois University Press, 1968), 19. Two other useful anthologies are Hennig Cohen and William B. Dillingham, eds., *Humor of the Old Southwest* (Boston: Houghton Mifflin, 1964), and B. A. Botkin, ed., *A Treasury of Mississippi River Folklore* (New York: Crown Publishers, 1955). M. Thomas Inge, ed., *The Frontier Humorists: Critical Views* (Hamden, CT.: Archon Books, 1975) is a good introduction to scholarship concerning this field. The most ambitious general study of southwestern humor remains Kenneth S. Lynn, *Mark Twain and Southwestern Humor* (Boston: Little, Brown, 1960). However, in many ways, Moore's *The Frontier Mind*, a study of Kentucky literature, includes the sharpest social analysis of this genre. Two recent essays review the modern criticism of this humor: Neil Schmitz, "Tall Tale, Tall Talk: Pursuing the Lie in Jacksonian Literature," *American Literature* 48 (1977): 471–91; Leland Krauth, "Mark Twain: The Victorian of Southwestern Humor," *American Literature* 54 (1982): 368–84.

4. Cohen and Dillingham, *Humor of the Old Southwest*, xi–xii; Morris W. Yates, *William T. Porter and the Spirit of the Times* (Baton Rouge: Louisiana State University Press, 1957).

5. Moore, *The Frontier Mind*, 74. Pascal Covici, Jr., argues that these narrative techniques "were used to accommodate the Gentlemen's need for low behavior from which to disassociate himself," *Mark Twain's Humor: The Image of a World* (Dallas: Southern Methodist University Press, 1962), 4–5.

6. Timothy Flint, *Recollections of the Last Ten Years* (Boston: Cunnings, Hilliard, and Company, 1826), 78.

7. Charles Joseph Latrobe, *The Rambler in North America*, 2 vols. (London: Harper & Brothers, 1835), reprinted in *Before Mark Twain*, 38.

8. Joseph Leathley Cowell, *Thirty Years Passed among the Players in England and America* (New York: Harper & Brothers, 1844), reprinted in *Before Mark Twain*, 65.

9. William C. Hall, "Reminiscence of Natchez-Under-the-Hill," *New York Spirit of the Times* 13 (December 11, 1843): 523, reprinted in *Before Mark Twain*, 199.

10. J. L. McConnel, *Western Characters or Types of Border Life in the Western States* (New York: Redfield, 1853).

11. W. P. Strickland, *The Pioneers of the West: Or, Life in the Woods* (New York: Carlton & Phillips, 1856), 199, 201.

12. Nathaniel B. Bishop, *Four Months in a Sneak-Box: A Boat Voyage of 2600 Miles Down the Ohio and Mississippi Rivers, and along the Gulf of Mexico* (Boston: Charles D. Dillingham, 1879), 58–66.

13. Maria R. Audubon, ed., *Audubon and His Journals* (London: John C. Nimmo, 1897), 2:443–49. This tale is undated, and was probably written between 1823 and 1843. Also see Donald Culross Peattie, *Audubon's America* (Cambridge: The Riverside Press, 1940), 125.

14. James W. Goodrich, "Robert Ormsby Sweeny: Some Civil War Sketches," *Missouri Historical Review* 77 (January 1983): 167.

15. Letter of Colonel John Van Deusen, Springfield, Missouri, July 28,1861, to his father, Van Deusen Letters, Beinecke Library, Yale University.

16. William Phillips, *The Conquest of Kansas by Missouri and Her Allies* (Boston: Phillips, Sampson & Co., 1856), 29. Emphasis in the original.

17. Julia Louisa Lovejoy to the Concord, New Hampshire, (*Independent Democrat*, September 5, 1856, in *Kansas Historical Quarterly* 15 (May 1947): 131; Chicago *Tribune*, April 20, 1857; Boston *Liberator*, January 4, 1856; Milford, Massachusetts, *Practical Christian*, January 26, 1856. These passages and that from Phillips, note 16, can be found in Michael Fellman, "Rehearsal for the Civil War: Antislavery and Proslavery at the Fighting Point in Kansas, 1854–56," in Lewis Parry and Michael Fellman, eds., *Antislavery Reconsidered: New Perspectives on the Abolitionists* (Baton Rouge: Louisiana State University Press, 1979), 287–307. Also see Michael Fellman, "Julia Louisa Lovejoy Goes West," *The Western Humanities Review* 31 (Summer 1977): 227–242. It is fascinating to note that, in 1827, Timothy Flint had upbraided easterners for conceiving of the backwoodsman as "a kind of humanized Orang Outang, like my lord Monboddo's man, recently divested of the unsightly appendage of a tail." "The Kentuckian in New York," *Western Monthly Review* 1 (1827): 88, quoted in Moore, *The Frontier Mind*, 69. James Burnette (Lord Monboddo), 1714–1799, was an eccentric Scottish jurist and writer who believed that orangutans belonged to the human species, and had "not yet attained the uses of speech," *The Origin and Progress of the Language*, 6 vols. (Edinburgh: Menson, 1773–1792), 1:239, 272, and passim. Monboddo, who also believed man deteriorated in civilization, was widely ridiculed for his humanization of orangutans, and both Flint and Stearns may have become conscious of this particular bestial reduction of humans through reading attacks on Monboddo's theory in the popular press. In addition, Dr. Samuel Johnson fumed obsessively to Boswell about Monboddo's theories. Flint may have read Boswell's *Life*, and also Johnson's letter to Mrs. Thrale: "[Monboddo is] the Scotch Judge who has lately written a strange book about the origins of the language, in which he traces monkeys up to men, and says that in some countries the human species have tails like other beasts. He inquired for these longtailed Men of [Sir Joseph] Banks, and was not pleased that they had not been found in all his peregrinations," letter of August 25, 1773, in R. W. Chapman, ed., *The Letters of Samuel Johnson* (Oxford: Clarendon Press, 1952), 1:344.

18. Testimony of O. S. Fahnstock, sergeant of Hopkins Battery, October 10, 1863, Two or More Name Citizen File, Department of the Missouri, Record Group 393, File 2637, National Archives, Washington. Emphasis in the original.

19. Leavenworth, Kansas, *Weekly Herald* 2, December 8, 1855; March 29, July 19, August 30, September 13, 1856, quoted in "Rehearsal for the Civil War," 299–302.

20. William Least Heat Moon, *Blue Highways: A Journey into America* (Boston: Little, Brown, 1982).

21. Mark Twain, "The Private History of a Campaign That Failed," in Justin Kaplan, ed., *Great Short Works of Mark Twain* (New York: Harper & Row, 1967), 145–47, 159, 161.

5

Robert E. Lee

MYTH AND MAN

TWO YEARS PRIOR TO DELIVERING this paper I published *The Making of Robert E. Lee*, and so I had had my say on this southern patrician general who had been transformed into the most highly mythicized icon of the Lost Cause. While writing that book, I had taken it as my charge to separate the historical figure from the mythic construction and to deal with each without confusing them. Whereas most Lee biographers—with the notable exceptions of Tom Connelley and Alan Nolan, whose original and critical work inspired me—had tended to admiration and even adulation for a man they considered a true hero, I intentionally remained as cool and detached as I could from the grandly redeeming narrative of the tragic hero. As a practicing historian I disbelieve in heroes, searching as I do to understand the motives and actions of human beings rather than to present stylized paragons of good or evil.

The concrete circumstances of the lecture invitation that elicited this essay had a great deal to do with how I shaped its content. I did not want to reprise the argument of my biography but to challenge my anticipated audience with a set of ideological as well as biographical issues that would penetrate the standard view of the Marble Man, Robert E. Lee.

In the spring of 2002, my long-time friend Bertram Wyatt-Brown invited me to give a paper at the Douglas Southall Freeman Conference— to be held jointly with the meeting of the Southern Intellectual History Group—taking place at the University of Richmond, where Bert held a visiting chair. I was asked to speak at a plenary session on Robert E. Lee that would take place on the floor of the Tredegar Iron Works, the most

Portions of this chapter were first published in Wallenstein, Peter, and Bertram Wyatt-Brown, eds. *Virginia's Civil War*. Charlottesville: University of Virginia, 2004.

important armaments facility of the Confederacy, then in the process of being turned into a museum. The location could not have been more symbolically freighted with white southernism, as the Richmond journalist Douglas Southall Freeman's three-volume Lee biography, published in the mid-1930s, had codified the myth of the Marble Man to which all subsequent biographers had to respond.

Knowing that I would be in the very heartland of the Lee legend, I also anticipated that my audience—around 400 people as it turned out—would most likely be almost entirely white, and mostly middle-aged or older, well-educated members of the upper middle-class of the former capital of the Confederacy. I knew that such folks had been raised during the segregation era, that they would have been schooled on the Freeman version of the Lee myth, and, more generally, on the nobility of the Lost Cause. Few of them would be extremist neo-Confederates, fulminating against the perfidious Yankee, or un-Reconstructed segregationists who somehow regretted the passing of the caste system that had replaced slavery. Yet I wondered to what degree they had pondered just how comfortable most of them had been growing up in a segregated society of which they were the racial beneficiaries. Certainly cognizant of the evils of slavery, they may have been less thoughtful about the destructiveness of the subsequent white supremacist regime, most of which ended only in the 1960s. The venerated Lee that they had read about in their schoolbooks had been the ideological capstone of the white-dominated racial caste system in which they had been bred. My paper was designed to unsettle them, politely but unequivocally, compelling them to question the beliefs with which they had been raised—beliefs epitomized by the Lee legend. I regarded this invitation as a political opportunity not to be ignored.

The other speakers there at the Tredegar Works were southern white men in their sixties—they too had been schooled in the Lost Cause tradition, although all were racial liberals, critical of the southern history they studied. Thus I was, if a fellow professional historian, the token "Yankee."

This outsider status was highlighted by Lee biographer Emory M. Thomas. A native of Richmond teaching at the University of Georgia, he spoke at considerable length before me, taking the occasion to denounce my biography in rather personal terms as a study of what Lee was not, in contrast to his own correct version of Lee as he really was. I was so dumbfounded by this attack that I began to scribble a reactive new introduction. However, by the time it was my turn to speak, I realized that this audience, bred in concepts of honor, would almost certainly believe that Thomas was being personally rude to a guest, and that he had used *ad hominem* argumentative tactics unacceptable to southern gentlemen. Rather than answering in kind I would honor that code by ignoring the personal attack and make my case without rancor and without apology.

As I began to deliver my speech, the room went quite still. Thomas had prepared the way for the audience to see a frothing alien, and my argument did challenge them. No one heckled; no one asked an unpleasant question afterwards. In composing this talk, my belief was that if they listened, even in disbelief, many in this group would go home and think about what I said, and then perhaps read more and question more about what lay behind some of the reputedly most noble values of their cultural homeland.

Immediately after the session, at a reception in another part of the Iron Works, relatively few people seemed eager to talk with me. Three young women did, however, and one of them, who was black, insisted on buying me a drink. Bert came over and told me that the conservative financial underwriters of the conference were furious with me for coming down to Virginia and criticizing the most heroic southerner of all times, and I told him that I did not give a damn.

The next morning, the Southern Intellectual History Group, composed of about 150 professors and graduate students, reconvened at the university. Not knowing what to expect when I walked in the front door, I was pleasantly surprised to be greeted with considerable warmth. My inner emotions were rather mixed—annoying but unmistakably self-pitying feelings of "where were you last night" mingled with a rather immodest pride that I had handled a hot spot as well as I could (something that is certainly not true of me on many occasions). And I felt confirmed in my belief that given time to think it over, southern whites would be open to challenges. Irony, a touch of anger, pride, and relief jostled together, making for one of the most emotionally complex, edgy, and ultimately rewarding experiences of my life as a historian. I believed I had spoken out of my convictions.

I felt freedom.

"Robert E. Lee: Myth and Man"

"'Tell Hill he *must* come up. Strike the tent,' he said, and spoke no more." Douglas Southall Freeman took these lines uncritically from Col. William Preston Johnston's purportedly eyewitness account of the 1870 deathbed scene of President Robert E. Lee of Washington College. These were soul-stirring final words, but they would have been a physiological impossibility. Writing in the *Virginia Magazine of History and Biography* in 1990, five distinguished neurologists sifted all available evidence left by those closest to the deathbed. They concluded that, for the last two weeks of his life, following his massive stroke, Lee could utter only the occasional monosyllable, suffering as he did from abulia—literally absence of the will.[1]

This touching scene, on which generations of southern school children were raised, arose, in fact, from the need of many white southern leaders and ordinary citizens to believe that Robert E. Lee's death had to be beautiful and transcendent, because he was the very personification of the southern nation, the embodiment of unbending southern nationalism. This was the only acceptable style of death for the peerless leader.

By similar mythic necessity, many have wanted to believe that immediately after the war, when a black man had the effrontery to come down to the front of the church to take communion at St. Paul's Episcopal Church in Richmond, Robert E. Lee came down the aisle to share the flesh and the blood of Christ with him, thus demonstrating biracial peace. This story derives from two very dubious brief passages, written in the popular press in 1905, forty years after the supposed event. And even according to them, Lee was almost certainly shaming the black man rather than accepting him. But the demands of legend have overwhelmed the critical capacities of scholars who have retailed the story as gospel.[2]

Concerning Lee's transformation from a human to the chief Confederate monument, Thomas L. Connelly wrote in his brilliant analysis of the posthumous Lee legend, *The Marble Man:* "The ultimate rationale of this pure nation was the character of Robert E. Lee. The Lost Cause argument stated that any society which produced a man of such splendid character, must be right."[3] Not only did this beatification transpose Lee into sainthood, but it also made his a most *political* sainthood. This essay explores two aspects of that transformation. One aspect is the historical Lee's actual participation in the early, formative stages of the victorious postwar, post-Confederate nationalist movement that destroyed Reconstruction and recreated white supremacy as a segregationist caste system, one that would last nearly one hundred years. The other aspect is the posthumous uses made by others of Lee's heritage, transforming him into an extremely "living" and useful historical monument, precisely by denying his human qualities in the name of the paragon, the usable paragon of all the genteel virtues.

In 1868 the historical Lee had been drawn into the Democratic presidential campaign. William S. Rosecrans, who was deputized to White Sulphur Springs, where Lee summered with other ex-Confederate bigwigs, induced Alexander H. H. Stuart, the leading Virginia backroom politician of his day, to draft a campaign letter. Lee willingly affixed his name as head signatory, and over thirty others then added their signatures. The Democratic position was that the most conservative possible group of older southern leaders could and should be trusted with the restoration of power as the means to end Reconstruction. Traditional paternalism could be trusted, the letter asserted. "The idea that the Southern people are hostile to the negroes and would oppress them, if it were in their power to do so, is entirely unfounded. They have grown up in our midst, and we have been accustomed from childhood to look upon them with kindness."[4]

Not just idealism characterized white paternalism, however. In view of the practical need for black labor, the letter went on, "self-interest, if there were no higher motive, would therefore prompt the whites to protect blacks." And only white domination could form the basis of this interested and kind paternalism: "It is true that the people of the South, in common with a large majority of the people of the North and West, are, for obvious reasons, inflexibly opposed to any system of laws that would place the political power of the country in the hands of the negro race." This rigid opposition, the letter explained, stemmed not from "any enmity"—any deep-seated race hatred—but from a "deep-seated conviction" that blacks lacked the "necessary intelligence to make them safe repositories of political power. They would inevitably become the victims of demagogues who for selfish purposes would mislead them into serious injury of the public." Southern whites wanted peace and the res-toration of the Union—"relief from oppressive misrule"—based on a re-turn of what these gentlemen called the "birth-right of every American," that is to say the vote for disenfranchised ex-Confederates as for every other white man. After restoration, later called Redemption, the natural white ruling class would "treat the negro populations with kindness and humanity."[5]

The letter's language was moderate; the politics were not. White pa-ternalism was to be a free grant from above, rather than a negotiated compromise resulting from any kind of power sharing with blacks. By 1877, growing frustrated and bored with Reconstruction, and as a means to resolve the hung election of 1876, the Republicans would agree with the essential terms of this proposal, and so Reconstruction ended on the Redeemers' terms.

After the war, Lee was close to the two leaders of Redemption in Vir-ginia, Alexander H. H. Stuart and James B. Baldwin, both of whom lived in Staunton, just forty miles up the road from Lexington, where Lee re-sided after the war. Lee was a member of the conservative portion of the self-named Conservative coalition of ex-Whigs and Democrats that formed in Virginia in the late 1860s. At the moderate end was William Mahone, whose forces urged the acceptance of black suffrage as grounds for the early reclaiming of home rule. Adding an equivalent claim for the restoration of the vote to ex-Confederates, conservatives accepted black suffrage, and even opposed the nomination of a too-overt white racist for the governorship. Horace Greeley then brokered the deal with President U. S. Grant, and Virginia reentered the Union in 1870 without the full experience of a Reconstruction government.

Some historians have argued that Virginia experienced Reconstruc-tion later than other former Confederate states, after the 1879 rise to state control of the Readjuster Movement. William Mahone had been squeezed out of power by the Conservative coalition by the Bourbons to his right, including Lee's closest associates. They insisted on paying off Virginia's prewar debts (unpaid during the war) in full, and to do so starved public education, especially for blacks, and they required pay-ment of a poll tax as a condition of voting. When the Readjusters gained control of the state government, they cut the linkage of the poll tax to the vote, thus ending it as a disenfranchising device; funded education for blacks, who had voted for them; and slashed the state debt; while truly not sharing power with African Americans.[6] *This* was southern white moderation.

In this political formation, Lee was a conservative, not a moderate. Before his death, he had explicitly predicted that, once back in power, whites would squeeze blacks out of any and all meaningful political participation, and so they did. By the 1883 elections, the conservatives regrouped and drove Mahone and white moderation from power for the remainder of the nineteenth century and well into the twentieth.

In private, after the war, the publicly bland Lee was bitter in his states' rights southern nationalism. He was most open with his Parisian nephew, Edward Lee Childe, a real favorite of his, perhaps because Childe was at a safe, transatlantic distance. To Childe, Lee sometimes expressed what could only be considered angry and antidemocratic anti-Americanism about where Republicans were taking the nation. "The tendency seems to be one vast Government, sure to become aggressive abroad & despotic at home," Lee wrote in 1867, "and I fear it will follow that road which history tells us such Republics have trod, might is believed to be right & the popular clamor the voice of God. . . . The greatest danger is the subversion of the old form of government and the substitution in its place of a great consolidated central power [that will] trample upon the reserved rights of the states & in time annihilate the Constitution."[7]

As well as being fundamentally opposed to postwar American nationalism, Lee was often antiblack. For example, in 1868 he wrote to his youngest son, Robert E. Lee, Jr., "you will never prosper with the blacks, and it is abhorrent to a reflecting mind to be supporting and cherishing those who are plotting & working for your injury, and all of whose sympathies and associations are antagonistic to yours. . . . Our material, social and political interests are naturally with the whites."[8] In the late 1860s, Lee pushed for black deportation and white immigration, as did many Virginia planters and industrialists, hoping for what one historian has called the immigration panacea. But in 1868, of 213,000 predominantly northern and western European immigrants to the United States, exactly 713 moved to Virginia.[9] Few Europeans wanted to hazard settling in the impoverished and violent postwar South. And black southerners did not simply go away either. Men like Lee, who wished they would, never formulated a plan for voluntary or forced black migration, but the wish was there that they would simply depart.

Thus, after the war, Lee was never apolitical. He participated actively in the rebirth of southern white nationalism, albeit in the *public* role of the austere senior statesman above the fray. But even better political uses of him by this cause could be made after his death, when the story was reformulated to insist that Lee had been entirely above politics. Politics are a mess, politicians are dogs, and, contrarily, the expression of supposedly eternal values is central for political movements, particularly revolutionary or counterrevolutionary ones. As Thomas Connelly has written, a pure man purified the Lost Cause. For the cult of Lee, the best text is Edward V. Valentine's 1883 white marble statue of Lee at the burial shrine in Lexington, lying not dead but asleep on the field of eternal battle, booted and with a sword at his side, in full Confederate uniform, forever ready to awaken and defend his people.

Two more texts, both taken from a public meeting in Richmond, twelve days after his death, demonstrate how quickly Lee was turned into a demigod. (By the way, Lee was a reserved man and would have detested this adulatory oratory.) Jubal T. Early, perhaps the leading ex-Confederate propagandist of the Lost Cause, strode to the platform and declared: Lee's "fame belongs to the world and to history, and [a] sacred duty devolves upon those whom, in defense of a cause he believed to be just, and to which he remained true to the latest moment of his life, and led so often to battle," to honor him appropriately. "We owe it to our fallen comrades, to ourselves, and to posterity, by some suitable and lasting memorial, to manifest to the world, for all time to come, that we were not unworthy to be led by our immortal chief, and [are] not now ashamed by the principles for which Lee fought." And then it was Jefferson Davis's turn to speak. More important than Lee's brilliant career, said Davis, were "his immortal qualities that rose to the height of his genius." Among these was "self-denial—always intent on the one idea of duty—self-control." Davis concluded: "This good citizen, this gallant soldier, this great general, this true patriot, had yet a higher praise than this—he was a true Christian."[10]

Here was light itself, and the destruction of Reconstruction had both light and dark sides, inextricably bound together in an understood if unstated political dialectic. There was the paramilitary, or terrorist, branch and the legitimist branch, which worked together by inference—mutually understood inference (and sometimes more overtly)—to achieve a common goal, power. The legitimist branch, run by gentlemen of station and honor, promised kind paternalism once white power was secured (secured by any means necessary; *that* was the inference). The redeemed regime would not be biracial, but top down in its protection of blacks on the part of unchallenged white authority. This kinder side of redemption was not untrue, as these men meant what they said, but it was always reinforced, whenever necessary, by the dark side, by force, whether in everyday acts of discrimination or in threats, or in various forms of violence, culminating in lynching, an increasingly common practice in the post-Reconstruction South.

However, *deniability* remained all-important, both for psychological reasons and for the political need to maintain the aura of justice. Others—trashy whites—did the lynching, while good whites would always be kind to blacks if only left alone to be so. This combination of light and dark was to remain true well into my lifetime, and I am not that old. Only black action and outside pressure ended segregation—it did not wither of itself. Left to their own devices, southern white liberals —and more-conservative paternalists—forever failed to escape the embrace of Southern white reaction, failed to establish a moderate biracial alternative.

This was a Southern nationalist movement, like many other separatist movements, and yet to a considerable degree it became American and not just southern. This can be seen, for example, in the 1884 election of Grover Cleveland, an understudied event. This first Democratic president elected since 1856 brought many ex-Confederates into powerful positions in his inner circle of advisers, his cabinet, and the Supreme Court, as they had already regained immense power in Congress. By 1896 the Supreme Court would legitimate formal segregation, and in 1898 a splendid little war reunited southern and northern warriors in a vigorous new American imperialism. Protestant northerners, afraid of waves of Jewish and Catholic immigrants, of labor strife, of wild urbanization, saw real virtues in the modes of southern white rule over their lower orders, and made more overt alliance with the Bourbons.[11]

In this process, Lee was also nationalized. Men on both sides of the Civil War, the argument ran, had been honorable, brave, and true to their beliefs, and Lee had been the first among this vast brigade, peaceful, always conciliatory, disinterested, duty-bound, noble—in sum, the pure American hero after all. This deracination of Lee from his historical context of rebellion and resistance was all mythic, all historically inaccurate, and all ideologically indispensable. Not coincidentally, the height of the Lee cult, roughly 1890 to 1930, was also the nadir of race relations and the black experience in postslavery America.

Finally, this ideologically useful Lee was most impressive when wrapped in the myth of the tragic Lee—according to which he had sacrificed all save honor for the defense of slavery and for secession, in neither of which he believed. Duty overcame personal judgment, this argument goes, as if this would have been a virtue. In *The Making of Robert E. Lee*, I have analyzed Lee's single serious statement on slavery, made in 1856, which I found to be old-fashioned for its day, an argument defending slavery as a necessary evil, as opposed to the argument that slavery was a positive good, the more radical and more common late-antebellum proslavery proposition. Someday, slavery would be extinguished, according to Lee, but God moved slowly: "While we see the course of the final abolition of human slavery is onward, & we give it the aid of our prayers & all justifiable means in our power, we must leave the progress as well as the result in His hands who sees the end; who chooses to work by slow influences; and with whom two thousand years are but a single day."[12]

Such fatalism, such inevitable and almost infinite postponement of abolition, was a proslavery position, not antislavery in the context of the United States in 1856. Moreover, when push came to shove, along with the rest of the Virginia gentry class, Lee went without doubt, hesitation, or later regret with those of his blood and marrow, with Virginia, the South, the plantation class, the white race. The bolder and harsher leaders of antebellum southernism, the fire-eaters, had banged the drum in 1861, and then the softer and more genteel gentlemen marched into war bound together with them. So it would be during the destruction of Reconstruction, with the gallant Lee posthumously still turned to the task, as the chief and fully disembodied spiritual avatar of southern white-supremacist nationalism.

Robert E. Lee: Appendix

Biographers of Lee and historians of Virginia and the Civil War continue to draw on a document dating from 1905, and they differ in their understandings of the event reported therein. Whether the four key individuals in the story all attended the church service in question is uncertain, as is whether they actually did or observed what is reported in the document —just as the interpretations are divergent. The document is generally said to have been "reprinted," but the two versions differ in intriguing ways. Both carry the title "Negro Communed at St. Paul's Church." The paired documents offer glimpses of various Virginians' Civil War, as experienced in the 1860s or as recalled four decades later.

The *Richmond Times-Dispatch* of April 16, 1905, carried this version, on page B5:

> Colonel T. L. Broun, of Charleston, W. Va., is in the city stopping on Floyd Avenue. He was present at St. Paul's Church just after the war, when a negro marched to the communion table ahead of the congregation.
>
> Colonel Broun, in speaking of the matter yesterday, said:
>
> "Two months after the evacuation of Richmond, business called me to Richmond for a few days, and on Sunday morning, in June, 1866, I attended St. Paul's Church. Dr. Minnegerode preached to a congregation fairly good. It was communion day. When the minister was ready to administer the Holy Communion, amongst those who first arose and advanced to the communion table was a tall, well dressed negro man, very black. He walked with an air of military authority. This was a great surprise and shock to the communicants and others present, who frequented that most noted of the Episcopal Churches in Virginia. Its effect upon the communicants was startling, and for several moments they retained their seats in solemn silence, and did not move, being deeply chagrined at this attempt of the Federal authorities, to offensively humiliate them during their most devoted church services. Dr. Minnegerode looked embarrassed.
>
> "General Robert E. Lee was present, and he, ignoring the action and very presence of the negro, immediately arose, in his usual dig-

nified and self-possessed manner, walked up the aisle of the church to the chancel rail and reverently knelt down to partake of the communion and not far from where the negro was.

"This lofty conception of duty by General Lee, under such provoking and irritating circumstances, had a magic effect upon the other communicants, who immediately went forward to the communion table. I, being one of the number, did likewise.

"By this action of General Lee, the services were concluded, as if the negro had not been present. It was a grand exhibition of superiority shown by a true Christian and great soldier under the most trying offensive circumstances."

A few months later, the following piece reappeared in *Confederate Veteran* (August 1905): 360:

Colonel T. L. Broun, of Charleston, W. Va., writes of having been present at St. Paul's Church, Richmond, Va., just after the war when a negro marched to the communion table ahead of the congregation. His account of the event is as follows:

"Two months after the evacuation of Richmond business called me to Richmond for a few days, and on a Sunday morning in June, 1865, I attended St. Paul's Church. Dr. Minnegerode preached. It was communion day; and when the minister was ready to administer the holy communion, a negro in the church arose and advanced to the communion table. He was tall, well-dressed, and black. This was a great surprise and shock to the communicants and others present. Its effect upon the communicants was startling, and for several moments they retained their seats in solemn silence and did not move, being deeply chagrined at this attempt to inaugurate the 'new regime' to offend and humiliate them during their most devoted Church services. Dr. Minnegerode was evidently embarrassed.

"Gen. Robert E. Lee was present, and, ignoring the action and presence of the negro, arose in his usual dignified and self-possessed manner, walked up the aisle to the chancel rail, and reverently knelt down to partake of the communion, and not far from the negro. This lofty conception of duty by Gen. Lee under such provoking and irritating circumstances had a magic effect upon the other communicants (including the writer), who went forward to the communion table.

"By this action of Gen. Lee the services were conducted, as if the negro had not been present. It was a grand exhibition of superiority shown by a true Christian and great soldier under the most trying and offensive circumstances."

LEE'S POSTHUMOUS CANONIZATION was contingent on his being recast as a tragic figure, who, the story goes, cast his lot with the Confederacy even though he was opposed to both secession and to slavery, and who, after the war, rose above divisiveness of race and section to present a healing vision for former Confederates and Americans more generally. Saint Robert served as proof that the Lost Cause had been noble and true. Anyone could win a struggle, but only the truly enlightened could fight powerfully for the right ends and then survive defeat in spiritual superiority. In my book, and much more concisely in this speech, I sought to question each element of the transcendental and heroic portrait of the Man and the Cause. Rather than reducing Lee the historical actor, for whom I had considerable sympathy, I tried to separate him from what had been made of him in what was still the widely accepted version of the maximum southern hero.

The myth of the Marble Man, like the wider myth of the Lost Cause, was a romantic abstraction. As the tale went, Lee had only fought in defense of his home state, Virginia. After the war he stood above politics for racial and national reconciliation. In the Lost Cause ideology, masters had been kind and slavery benign, and secession and civil war had been a response to northern aggression by defenders of states' rights and liberty. The Confederacy had lost only because of northern material and manpower superiority, and the segregation system was a traditionalist defense of the natural, and good, social order.

Beneath these shining beliefs lay the bigoted certainties of white supremacy that licensed the use of violence when necessary to "defend" the superior race against the inferior but always threatening under race. Even in our day, a majority of southern whites will defend the more encoded portions of the Lost Cause—the sort who keep the Confederate battle flag waving on the lawn of the South Carolina legislature. The Lost Cause has on the whole gone deep underground, at least until "tradition" and "heritage" need protecting. Just what that heritage might be on the material place is not explained—but, after all, the Lost Cause always has existed on the spiritual level, the true plane of inner and higher moral life.

In addition to quoting selectively from an 1856 letter in which Lee regretted the existence of slavery—but also renounced any abolitionist inferences from his position—most practitioners of the Lee mythos nearly always cite the famous, although poorly documented, postwar incident in which Lee took communion next to a black man. For example, Emory Thomas, in his talk preceding mine, stated, "Lee attempted to redeem awkward circumstances, and bring grace. At St. Paul's Church, in Richmond, in June 1865, a very large black man first responded to the call for receive communion. Gasp. No one moved, except Lee, who walked forward and knelt beside him." Thomas here paraphrased Douglas Southall Freeman to demonstrate that Lee had risen above racism as the true gentleman, although even here Thomas's characterization of the black man as "very large" connotes a threatening quality about his intrusive and unwelcome presence, a traditional race-based fear.

When I spoke I did not have the primary text from which this spiritually redemptive interpretation was extrapolated. The morning after I presented my talk, as the Southern Intellectual History Group reconvened, professor Phillip J. Schwartz of Virginia Commonwealth University, a member of St. Paul's Church, handed me the two versions of the 1905 document that are the sole evidence of this incident, written forty years after the event, which I have attached to this essay. According to the only witness, Colonel T. L. Broun, "By this action of Gen[.] Lee the services were conducted as if the negro had not been present. It was a grand exhibition of superiority shown by a true Christian and great soldier under the most trying and offensive circumstances." We do not learn if the black man kneeling at the alter was given the Eucharist, nor whether Lee offered a Christian and genteel southern welcome to him after the service—both of which would have demonstrated racial reconciliation and Lee's personal grace. If the lone witness it to be believed, the black man was almost certainly shunned as a reprehensible outsider. Therefore this incident is a very fragile reed on which to hang an argument about Lee as a welcoming racial liberal, particularly when so many other actual statements of his reflected not biracial acceptance but the sometimes vehement racism common to his place and class.

The starting point for my reconsideration of the historical Lee was my unromantic but to me commonsensical belief that he was a conventional member of the Virginia gentry class of his time. The title of my biographical study, *The Making of Robert E. Lee,* was a class inversion of the title of E. P. Thompson's seminal study, *The Making of the English Working Class.* Whereas Thompson had developed his understanding of class formation in the activities and the consciousness of early nineteenth-century English workers, I was trying to reconstruct class formation by analyzing the mentality and behavior of a charter member of the most self-assertive, rich, and powerful upper class in American history. Lee ought not to be analyzed as rising above his station to some sort of ahistorical super-humanity, I believed, but rather as rising to leadership within his class, trying to represent the best they professed to offer while sharing in their fundamental beliefs, fears, and hopes. He did not set himself against white Virginia, but jettisoned his American citizenship and his oath of allegiance as an army officer when confronted with the clear alternative of rejecting his deepest identity as a white Virginia gentleman. He was to me a class exemplar rather than a tragic figure, consistent in his deepest values, which he affirmed rather than contradicted by his life choices, before and after the Civil War.

Lee regretted slavery in the abstract, but when compelled to choose sides in 1861, he did so without much discernable agony and without ever looking back. This was common to many if not most of his fellow southern white conservatives when secession and civil war hit them in the face. Was it tragic, or, as I never said in so many words, cowardly and even rather stupid for them to go along with their section and let themselves be stampeded by the radical reactionaries they then joined to form the Confederacy? On the whole the traditional conservative leadership cadre that had resisted secession took over the Confederacy, both the army and the state apparatus, pushing the more rabid demagogues to the side. Nevertheless they followed the lead of the fire-eaters when seceding and entering the war, and after it they joined with the most extreme political elements of their race to create and sustain a segregationist regime that was always demeaning to African Americans, and, whenever whites deemed it necessary, deeply violent.

Almost nothing had been written about Lee's postwar political engagement: he was reified by biographers and Lost Cause practitioners as supposedly above the fray, serving in his bucolic college presidential retreat to return calm to the South by magnificent, silent example. In fact his political ties to Alexander H. H. Stuart, an Old Whig who had served as secretary of the interior in the Millard Fillmore cabinet, and Stuart's brother-in-law, James B. Baldwin, were sustained and significant. These other men had been reluctant secessionists who nevertheless played important roles in the Confederate rebellion, and after the war they formed the "Committee of Nine," a broad-based conservative movement that ended Reconstruction in Virginia in 1870, almost before it began, with Lee's participation and public endorsement. Discussion of this political activity had been almost entirely missing in the major Lee biographies, which cast him as a transcendent peacemaker and racial reconciliationist. My task was to ground Lee in his own social, political, and racial milieu, a place he certainly knew he inhabited and served. In common with his class, he took as his postwar task not to retreat and placate northern sentiment but to regroup and retake unchallenged political and social power in the South.

Should the fate of the more genteel elements of this white ruling class be considered tragic? I believe that the term "tragic" ought to be applied instead to the African American population that group oppressed, whether or not they found the extreme measures that reinforced the segregation system rather too distasteful to think about honestly, much less to oppose. That is why I made the need for "deniability" so central to my argument. To question Lee was to question the whole southern white social construct, with white gentlemen in unquestioned command. In many respects it amazed me that what I said remained controversial among well-educated people in Richmond, Virginia, in 2002. Somewhere, beneath the surface, the ancien regime still lives on as an unacknowledged mentality; whether consciously or not, the need for deniability continues.

The Marble Man and the (still) Lost Cause, are often treated as if their historical and mythical reconstructions are both unique to one time and place, and timelessly universal in their religious implications. Myth-making elevates exceptionalism to a spiritual realm, where historical figures and their values are transvaluated—elevated above human contradictions to godly purity and timelessness. The Lee shrine at Washington and Lee University is a physical manifestation of this transcendental symbol of the imperishable (white) South.

Although I failed to deal with the Lee problem in an overtly comparative framework, other historical experiences provided a backdrop for my thinking about this case. Living in Canada, I have learned a great deal about separatist nationalism from the Quebec experience. Quebec nationalists have their Lost Cause—the military defeat of the French by the English on the Plains of Abraham in 1757—and they have constructed a pantheon of hero figures, a national linguistic and ethnic project, and a compelling need for independence and liberty akin to southernism. Nationalism can carry great weight even if a society does not separate politically, or even if rebellion has failed on the material level of reality. The Quebec experience and that of Catalonia, Scotland, and Wales, to take other examples, have taught me much about nationalism without a nation state—much like the postwar South, where nationalist ideology led to a seizure of governmental power on white terms that the rest of the American nation, including the Supreme Court, accepted for nearly a century.

In addition, also implicitly, the Irish experience was highly instructive to my thinking about the two-tier mode of postwar retaking of political power in the South. For decades in Ireland, the paramilitary branch—the IRA terrorists—worked hand in glove with the legitimist Sean Fein arm of a national liberation movement, as both struggled for shared political goals. One faction fought while the other negotiated, but the ends were shared and each party understood the task of the other, whether inferentially or through actual discussions. Clearly, in the postwar South, Lee was of the legitimist party: he never would have called for the use of political violence that was central to the destruction of Reconstruction and the "redemption" of his native region. However, it is notable that he was silent on the growing violence of the postwar South, just has he had never condemned or even acknowledged the slaughter of African American Union troops after the Battle of the Crater in 1864, although he was standing nearby when it happened. He agreed with the goal of white power and, in tandem with other men of his class, turned a blind eye to its most violent manifestations.

A more explicitly comparative approach to Lee and his contexts would reveal some of the ways in which the ideological and mythological processes of both the Confederate and the racially segregated postwar South fit wider historical and narrative traditions. I went down this path only by inference in my study of Lee, thus contributing to a sense of the unique despite my purpose to concentrate on the conventional. I felt compelled to engage the basic issues at hand in as direct a manner as possible in order to destabilize a traditional version of a man and his times, whereas a comparative approach might have aided historical revision in a larger sense.

My focus in my work on Lee was essentially biographical, and one limit of that form of historical writing is the seemingly inevitable tendency to explore historical context primarily as background to the unfolding story of a dramatic life. On the other hand, Lee was at the mythical apex of a whole culture that was undergoing crisis, and so analyzing him implied questioning the aspirations and experiences of his culture as a whole. Symbols really count, and discussing the Marble Man while also dealing with the struggling human being masked by his legend was perhaps a sufficient reason for writing about Lee. I also was aware, of course, that more readers would be attracted to a biographical study of Lee than to a broader and more diffuse discussion of the patrician class in nineteenth-century Virginia. That choice pleased Bob Loomis, my editor at Random House (and thus me too), and allowed me to argue as best I could about the Virginia gentry through one example rather than as a whole. Perhaps this was in part a business decision dictated by the market, but it also made political sense to reach as broad a readership as possible with controversial work. Sometimes it is difficult to separate idealism from cynicism.

NOTES

1. William Preston Johnson, "Death of General Lee," in *Personal Reminiscences of General Robert E. Lee*, ed. J. William Jones (New York: D. Appleton, 1875), 451; Douglas Southall Freeman, *R. E. Lee* (New York: Scribner's, 1934–35), 4:492; Marvin P. Rozear, E. Wayne

Massey, Jennifer Horner, Erin Foley, and Joseph C. Greenfield, Jr., "R. E. Lee's Stroke," *Virginia Magazine of History and Biography* 97 (April 1990): 291–308.

2. Col. T. L. Broun, of Charleston, West Virginia, as quote in the *Richmond Times-Dispatch*, April 16, 1905, and the *Confederate Veteran* 13 (August 1905): 360. Colonel Broun thought Lee's act (assuming it did take place) was conducted "as if the negro had not been present. It was a grand exhibition of superiority shown by a true Christian and great soldier under the most trying and offensive circumstances." It is revealing to compare the white supremacist original with Emory Thomas's romantic interpretation of this source: "Another person arose from the pew and . . . knelt near the black man and so redeemed the circumstance. This grace-bringer, of course, was Lee," whose "actions were far more eloquent than anything he spoke or wrote." Quoted in *Robert E. Lee: A Biography* (New York: W. W. Norton & Company, 1995), 372. Readers are urged to consult the documents from 1905, which appear in the appendix to this essay.

3. Thomas L. Connelly, *The Marble Man: Robert E. Lee and His Image in American Society* (Baton Rouge: Louisiana State University Press, 1977), 94.

4. Lee to William S. Rosecrans, August 26, 1868, Robert E. Lee Papers, Virginia Historical Society.

5. Ibid.

6. For postwar Virginia politics, see Michael Fellman, *The Making of Robert E. Lee* (New York: Random House, 2000), 264–94; Jack P. Maddex, Jr., *The Virginia Conservatives, 1867–1879* (Chapel Hill: University of North Carolina Press, 1979); Maddex, "Virginia: The Persistence of Centrist Hegemony," in *Reconstruction and Redemption in the South,* ed. Otto H. Olsen (Baton Rouge: Louisiana State University Press, 1980), 113–55; and Richard Lowe, *Republicans and Reconstruction in Virginia, 1856–70* (Charlottesville: University Press of Virginia, 1991). For Mahone, see Jane Dailey, *Before Jim Crow: The Politics of Race in Postemancipation Virginia* (Chapel Hill: University of North Carolina Press, 2000), and the still valuable Nelson M. Blake, *William Mahone of Virginia: Soldier and Political Insurgent* (Richmond, VA: Garret & Massie, 1935).

7. Lee to Edward Lee Childe, January, 5 1867, Lee Papers, Jesse Ball Dupont Library, Stratford Hall Plantation, Stratford, Virginia.

8. Lee to Robert E. Lee, Jr., March 12, 1868, quoted in *The Recollections and Letters of Robert E. Lee,* ed. Robert E. Lee, Jr. (New York: Doubleday, Page, 1904), 306.

9. Maddex, *Virginia Conservatives,* 178–83.

10. Addresses of J. A. Early and Jefferson Davis to the Surviving Officers of the Army of Northern Virginia, Lynchburg, October 24, 1870, in Jones, *Reminiscences,* 334, 340–41.

11. This discussion of the destruction of Reconstruction and the triumph of white supremacy as the culmination of the era of the Civil War is fleshed out in Michael Fellman, Lesley J. Gordon, and Daniel E. Sutherland, *"This Terrible War": The Civil War and Its Aftermath* (New York: Longman, 2002), 346–82.

12. Fellman, *Making of Robert E. Lee,* 72–74. For the full text of this letter from Lee to his wife, Mary Curtis Lee, December 27, 1856, see Freeman, *Lee,* 1:371–73.

6

Reflections on *Inside War*

AFTER THE CIVIL WAR, northern veterans formed the Grand Army of the Republic, which served as a powerful lobby to demand pensions for those who fought—the first major use of the national government for social welfare expenditures—and to build clubhouses for fellowship, celebration, and Republican Party politicking. Veterans constructed temples to their belief in the triumph of the Union cause, which reaffirmed the United States' position, as Abraham Lincoln had put it, as the bastion of freedom, as a light unto the nations.

Surely, therefore, the posh and overstuffed Union League Club in Philadelphia was the appropriate place to hold the first conference of the Society of Civil War Historians. Until recently, membership in the club was restricted to men who were professing Republicans. Many of us at the conference responded to the ironies as well as the logic of choosing this locale for our meeting. For the conference, Lesley Gordon, a member of the program committee, had arranged for a panel discussion to mark the twentieth anniversary of the publication of *Inside War*. The other presenters were John Inscoe and Paul Anderson, both of whom discussed the myriad implications of guerrilla warfare in that book, in their work, and in scholarship yet to come.

Coincidentally, a few months after this session had been planned, but before it took place, the learned and provocative historian Mark Neely published *The Civil War and the Limits of Destruction*, a book that roundly criticized *Inside War* and subsequent work, not only on guerrilla warfare in particular but on the social history of the Civil War in general. Thus

Portions of this chapter were presented to the conference of the Society of Civil War Historians, Philadelphia, June 15, 2008.

Neely set a framework for debating some central issues raised in the current discussion of the Civil War, a useful take-off point for our session.

"No other book has had more influence on the writing of Civil War history than . . . *Inside War*," Neely wrote. "Once a 'sideshow' . . . guerrilla warfare has stolen the show. [This book and the] vivid and innovative studies that followed the trail Fellman blazed have gone a long way toward giving the Civil War an appearance of remorselessness and grisly violence that respected no persons or property . . . Fellman has begun a little revolution in writing Civil War history." This revolution amounts, Neely regretted, to the promulgation of a "cult of violence" in historical interpretation, emphasizing the terrors of a civil war that was in fact, he repeatedly insisted, "restrained."

Missouri, the only site of guerrilla warfare he examined in his book, had in fact been a "sideshow [and such] savage attacks were an exception," to what he presumes to have been normal modes of combat in the war. In general, Neely concluded that Civil War Americans were "lucky" in this conflict and that "the country's bloodiest war pales in comparison" to wars elsewhere. Therefore, historians who promote the "cult of violence" argument have long "distorted at best" the impact of this civilized and limited war. Furthermore, *Inside War*—which he characterized as "gloomy"—and the guerrilla war literature that followed, he claimed, have been suspiciously driven by "a methodological imperative: the interests and methods of the New Social History . . . which for the first time brought the common people . . . into the pages of academic history books . . . and conversely began to crowd the generals and politicians out of them. . . . Guerrilla warfare had the essential quality needed for social history: it involved whole communities, not soldiers alone, but men, women, children, slaves and yeomen."

When one considers the continuing glut of books on the market about Abraham Lincoln and the great white generals (to which I have contributed), it is difficult to conclude that, at least on the popular level, Civil War history has been swept by social history. Indeed, one might argue that Civil War history is the single subdiscipline in American history that has been most resistant to social history. In part, this is due to the massive number of buffs who want to read about great men and battles, and to explore details about logistics, weapons, uniforms, and flags. Many readers seem to seek pleasure and reassurance that they can really understand the most important meanings of the Civil War while leaving troublingly contradictory political issues such as slavery, gender, and class on the margins of discussions, settling for an overarching patriotic gloss that the war advanced freedom and justice for all. Many historians have fed this appetite; indeed, the belief that the Civil War was less horrible than other wars—that it was consciously and nobly fought by the Union for high ideals of liberty and freedom that turned the war itself and Reconstruction that followed into the Second American Revolution —is now the credo of the quasiofficial Union Triumphalist school of Civil War studies.

Cultural history of the Civil War tends to zero in on the processes of war itself rather than asserting the notion that political outcomes justified the immense suffering and human loses. I am a very doubting Thomas when it comes to the insistence in traditional historical quarters that the war was characterized by soldierly ideological imperatives and that it "solved" the problems of slavery and racial injustice. Such idealistic abstractions strike me as opposite to the nature of the war one discovers in the archives and when digging into the experiences of ordinary people. In fact it provides a formula for overlooking the worst aspects of combat and military and civilian inhumanity by stressing that whatever the means, the results were worth it.

Luckily for us all, the Civil War is the best-documented war in American history. There was no military censorship of letters, and diary keeping was not proscribed, as was the case in later wars. Journalists gained almost free access to soldiers most all the time. And because this was the biggest event in the lives of most of the participants, civilian and soldier alike, huge reams of documents have survived in the archives. Some historians still base their conclusions on the multivolume postwar *War of the Rebellion* volumes, but this was an official record, selected by elderly Union war veterans interested in presenting their self-cleansing version of history decades after the war was over. Refreshingly, the new cultural historians have ransacked those archives while asking more complex and challenging questions about the everyday realities of Civil War America.

When working on *Inside War,* I spent a decade visiting the archives not only in Missouri but also in the surrounding states that sent soldiers into Missouri during the war. And I believe that I was the first historian to make full use of the records of the Department of the Missouri in the National Archives in Washington. There, tied up in red ribbons and sent off from Missouri at the end of the war, were thousands of depositions, court martial proceedings, and other records collected by Union provost marshals in every fortified county seat in a state run primarily by martial law. This amounted to a hugely documented laboratory (if poorly arranged in the National Archives) that revealed extraordinary complexities in the means by which infuriated fighters on both sides and their confused officers conducted the most brutal forms of war—it was about as far as you could get from the often-repeated tales of martial glory at battles like Gettysburg and Vicksburg.

In Philadelphia, partly in response to Mark Neely's critique, I sought to underline the methodological point that *Inside War* was intended to challenge master narratives of the Civil War by focusing instead on the human experiences of warfare. I sought to counter the practice of reducing the central meanings of the Civil War to an idealized set of moral ends that minimized or denied the horrific means of war for all those caught in its destructive grip. My effort was consciously antiromantic and hyperrealistic.

Later, in its February 2009 issue, *Civil War Times* published an edited version of my critique of Neely along with his spirited reply. But the original version of my paper, which was feistier and fuller, is the one printed here.

"Reflections on Inside War*"*

Using a metaphor more revealing than he may have intended, Mark Neely recently criticized John Keegan's seminal history of combat, *The Face of Battle,* because, in Neely's reckoning, it "began to write military history more from the point of view of the common soldier in the trench than from that of the general in his headquarters. The effect was naturally bloody, like touring a slaughterhouse rather than having a steak in the dining room of a meatpacking executive." This is a subsidiary historiographical aside in Neely's sustained criticism of *Inside War* and the social history of the Civil War for bringing what he calls a mythic "cult of violence" into Civil War studies.

I plead guilty as charged. If some more traditional military historians continue to write from the perspective of the general staff dining room, where war is alchemized into abstractions like restraint and discipline, many social historians of the Civil War indeed are down in the trenches, smeared with blood. For us, the Civil War was a gigantic, messy, decentralized affair, severing limbs from bodies, destroying hearts and minds.

Moreover, although it settled the issue of chattel slavery, neither the slaughterhouse of Civil War nor the political machinations of Reconstruction solved the underlying issue of racial justice. That was why Dan Sutherland, Lesley Gordon, and I ended our textbook not in 1877 but in 1896, the time by which a brutal white supremacist regime had devoured the South, and to which the American people, the national political system and, the Supreme Court had acquiesced. Dated that way, the political resolutions wrought by the war were ambiguous and limited. Certainly, a central political premise of *Inside War* was the belief that it behooves us to challenge the central thesis of the dominant Unionist Triumphalist school, which argues that the Civil War must have been a just war because it was morally reducible to a conscious crusade intended to eradicate slavery and further freedom and justice for all. To my mind, wartime and postwar political reconstruction were equivocal and relatively short-term affairs that did not result in genuine liberation for African Americans. The Whiggish argument about ever-increasing liberty and the inevitable triumph of democracy for all was *not* settled by the Civil War, however broadly construed.

What I intended when writing about Missouri was a pragmatic, empirically based escape from celebratory abstractions, plunging readers into the middle of the experience of war as it had been lived not merely by soldiers but by civilians as well. Guerrilla warfare was an obvious place to go to begin to broaden our understanding of the internal meanings of the Civil War, and through that route, the history of warfare more generally. I am honored if my effort stimulated the work of other historians who have deepened our understanding of the breadth and depth of guerrilla warfare, placing it into the center of the conflict of which it formed geographically the most widespread theaters. And I am glad to have helped erase the supposed line between the genders and between citizens and soldiers in a people's war.

This sense of experiential purpose in history writing emerged for me from living through and engaging against the war in Vietnam, and from the need to analyze the Holocaust—I would say my need to understand those horrific events created many of the emotional and intellectual imperatives that I brought to study of the Civil War. Far from being apologetic about plumbing and applying subjective responses to events I examine as an historian, I believe that self-consciousness of this sort can deepen our understanding, our compassion, and our criticism. We need to imagine ourselves into the trenches, the isolated farms, the putrid army camps and refugee camps, if we wish to reconstruct war as people experienced it, far from the high-brass dining room. And we can learn from all wars about what happens in each war, and apply those insights to conflicts past, present, and even future. (In this context I was reassured by one Civil War historian—although I do not remember which one it was—who, at a recent conference banquet, informed me that one of his students told him that *Inside War* sure seemed to be written with Iraq in mind. Of course, it had been Vietnam that had been behind my book, and I was also thinking of Ireland forever and of Bosnia at about the time that it appeared. But indeed Iraq fits along the continuum of civil and colonial wars.)

What I believe I was doing—and here my disclaimer is that my work is always more intuitive than programmatic, so I am not sure how clearly I was thinking at the time—was challenging the master narrative not only of the Civil War, but of America as the land of ever-unfolding liberty and justice for all. For the vital chunk of the national chronology of most concern to us in this room, that master narrative is clear—and here I am paraphrasing James McPherson, the most influential Civil War historian for general readers—that the Civil War was an ideologically driven, antislavery crusade responding to an ideologically driven, proslavery preemptive counterrevolution. Following the war (although beginning in 1863 with the Emancipation Proclamation), Reconstruction furthered the second American Revolution in freedom that the preemptive southern reactionary counterrevolution had been intended to prevent. And then? Then let's agree to stop in 1877, but take up the story in the 1950s and 60s, when Martin Luther King and the civil rights activists breathed new life into the Thirteenth, Fourteenth, and Fifteenth amendments, bringing forth in the land a glorious new step forward in the inexorable, if sometimes temporarily blocked, march of liberty.

But what of the near century of the dominance of a brutal and systematic white supremacy regime in the South, agreed to by northerners and even the Supreme Court? This era has become the longest footnote in American history. Or it has been softened, except by Leon Litwack, into an inferentially not-so-bad period of black institution building despite the institutions and practices of segregation. And in our own day, when we celebrate our progress toward freedom, we tend to forget or downplay the deeply racial distribution of poverty, violence, and incarceration.

Inside War in effect, if not completely consciously, was a counter proposition to this paean to American freedom. It was grounded in my utter skepticism about the use of military force for reform purposes, my disbelief that lofty and idealistic goals are matched by quotidian political means, much less military violence, and my sense that power and domination have more to do with nation-state and economic construction than do mantras about progress and freedom, highly advertised values that in fact are often rationalizations used by those with power and wealth.

This skepticism, which I believe needs to be applied ruthlessly by professional historians, in my case grows out of disillusioned liberalism. If I believed we could be self-organized without collective frameworks, I would be an anarchist, but I lack faith in inherent human perfectibility, whether communal or individual, or for that matter belief in the always self-correcting invisible hand of the so-called free market. If I believed in a naturally sufficient and permanent social organicism, I would be a conservative, but I don't believe that either. If I believed in original sin or if I were an utter cynic, I would just accept human depravity, but I do not believe that that is the whole story of individuals or societies. So I must fall back on the proposition that I developed while confronting the horrors of Missouri warfare: that we all have natural capacities for compassion as well as for destructiveness, that mutual aid as well as the most brutal slaughter both are fully human capacities and social constructions.

This sensibility is less than a theory, and in any event, in common with most historians I am not a theorist, but at most an applied theorist, a pragmatist. William James is my guide. We do not look, or ought not look, to discover systematic theories and apply them deductively, but to use them pragmatically, as tools for digging through immediate issues. Our generalizations tend to grow out of the specific rather than the other way around.

What I think I was doing in *Inside War*—and I see this a lot more clearly twenty years on—was to posit a form of historical social psychology as opposed to a progressive historical master narrative. By getting so up close and experiential, I was challenging the faith in abstractions about inevitable liberty and American exceptionalism more generally. I was arguing that Americans fight war, whether civil or colonial, in just as filthy a fashion as do other peoples. I was challenging the notion that high ideals had much to do with the fight itself when one really looked at combat as it existed out there in places like Missouri. And I was arguing that this was not an exception to so-called civilized warmaking but was the essence of warmaking itself, raw and red of tooth and claw.

I also realize more fully now than when I was writing, that I was arguing from a set of premises more universal than particular. Elsewhere [in chapter three of this book] I argue that the processes I found in Missouri were but one chapter of a book of war, with chapters from the Greeks and Romans to the Thirty Years' Wars, to the wars of religion, to Ireland and Yugoslavia, and for that matter to Rwanda, Darfur, and Iraq. Missouri was unexceptional.

This perspective ought to be projected backward to the American Revolutionary war. This was as much a civil war as an anticolonial war; most of it was fought not by stand-up armies but by militias and guerrillas and dispersed counterinsurgent troops. American historians of that period still seem on the whole wedded to the proposition that the American Revolution was a war of libertarian ideals, won, as John Adams said it, before the first shot was fired. This beautiful revolution is another big building block in an exceptionalist and abstract American idealism that looks past actual combat for the great and permanent ideals that the nasty wars presumably settled.

This brings me back to Mark Neely, who argues repeatedly that Americans fought the Civil War with discipline and restraint. Any deviations to the rule of restraint were merely exceptions to Neely. Thus guerrilla warfare—and he really only considers Missouri—was, in his words, a "sideshow." Thus Fort Pillow was an exception to the general rule of not shooting prisoners, although there is enough published work to suggest that wherever Confederates confronted black Union soldiers they usually shot prisoners and that the rules of race war accounted for this slaughter—rules that would later apply to systemic lynching, and not just from the 1880s, but in the Redeemers' successful paramilitary struggle to destroy Reconstruction. Not to mention, and Neely does not, the 56,194 prisoner-of-war deaths that Charles Sanders analyzes in his stunning book, *While in the Hands of My Enemies*. Sanders argues, and I would agree, that "Union and Confederate leaders knew full well that their policies and actions were resulting—*directly and unambiguously*—in the suffering and deaths of thousands of prisoners." Yes, the Civil War did not result in genocide, campaigns of rape, or population cleansing. No, the brutalities of that war were not exceptions to a rule of restraint.

In his otherwise realistic and compelling book, *The Hard Hand of War*, my friend Mark Grimsley, with whom I long have had a good-spirited debate, asserts quite out of the blue:

> If the Union's hard war effort displayed a novel element, it lay primar-
> ily with the linkage with a democratic society [that] made possible a
> politically and morally aware citizen soldiery capable of discrimina-
> tion and restraint as well as destruction. The Union volunteer who
> marched under Grant, Sherman, and Sheridan was a very different
> instrument than the ancien regime soldier . . . under Frederick the
> Great; for that matter, a different instrument even than contem-
> porary European soldiers. It was the peculiar nature of the Federal
> citizen-soldier—his civic mindedness, his continued sense of con-
> nection and community and public morality—that made possible the
> "directed severity." The Federal rank-and-file were neither barbarians,
> brutalized by war, nor "realists" unleashing indiscriminate violence.
> Their example holds out hope that the effective conduct of war need
> not extinguish the light of moral reason.

This statement reads to me like a proclamation of faith, an a priori assertion that American soldiers are fundamentally different than other

soldiers serving corrupt autocracies. Democrats born and bred, they escape, uniquely, the barbarism of becoming warriors. They service moral reason even in the throes of battle. This is a circular argument based on a belief in a morally improving American civil religion. Such American exceptionalism means that any act of barbarism by Americans fighting war is an exception to the rule of restraint and discipline that is essentially true of American soldiers, separated as they are from European soldiers. Even Neely believes that this posited democratic morality collapsed when white Americans fought the first Americans, something for which Grimsley's more categorical statement would not allow.

So when one goes to the archives and discovers not tailored officer's reports of the type that made in into the OR, but atrocities, does one conclude that these were un-American exceptions or sideshows, or aberrations of the wicked few? Or should one reconsider the religion of moralistic exceptionalism?

What then to make of the "cult of violence," as opposed to the war of restraint and discipline? Actually I do think that soldiers create a warrior's cult for themselves when they engage in the terrors, the suffering, killing, and dying of making war. I have been somewhat disappointed that few in Civil War history have followed this lead—although Drew Faust's magnificent new book on understanding death and killing really blazes new directions. Down in the encampments more digging is in order. There, soldiers revised their personalities and peacetime values into something quite different; Christianity, individualism, and Republicanism were reworked, as all major ideologies can be—to justify slaughter. Even deeper than that, the human and social desire to commit widespread destruction, torture and, atrocities—the part of my book that caused me the most grief—could be moved more fully into the center of discussions of the guerrilla war theaters of the Civil War. This heart of darkness is a central part of the way societies make war. By this token Abu Ghreib and Guantanamo Bay are not sideshows but hands-on applications of standard operating procedure, promulgated, even if somewhat indirectly, by the highest authorities.

Most Civil War discussions veer away into less immediately horrifying problems. It is really hard to think through such issues, although the archives are full of such accounts. And it is hard to get away from the master narrative about the Civil War as a just war, an antislavery crusade, which is what Americans want to believe about their better angels. Yet I argue that not only did the postwar period see a well-organized, violently racist, and successful southern white nationalist counterrevolution, the war itself was filled with racial ambiguities that made it something quite other than a fulfilling moral crusade, as Ira Berlin and his colleagues have demonstrated so convincingly in their documentary collections. Moreover, the corruptions of organized killing filtered back into the civil society from which the citizen soldiers had never fully departed. The brutalities of domination did not stop in 1865 or 1877.

What if war is inherently like that? What if "peace" is blurred with war? What is the sideshow and what is the real war? What if there is no gloriously libertarian master narrative? What if the United States is a nation among nations, an empire among empires? Are we capable of living with a tragic sensibility empty of the presumed upward trajectory toward a final meaning? Which sensibility is the more dangerous basis for our future actions when we analyze our past—tragedy or perpetually naïve idealism?

SINCE I WROTE THIS PAPER, Daniel E. Sutherland and Clay Mountcastle have each published an excellent synthesis of guerrilla warfare during the American Civil War. Many prior studies focused on a single region or state or outburst, and although both Sutherland, in *A Savage Conflict: The Decisive Role of Guerrillas in the American Civil War,* and Mountcastle, in *Punitive War: Confederate Guerrillas and Union Reprisals,* do considerable archival digging, each is intent on painting a broad historical canvas of guerrilla warfare right across the divided nation. Together, building on the wide range of scholarship that preceded them, they definitively establish that guerrilla war was central to the Civil War as a whole rather than constituting a sideshow. I believe that most scholars working in the field of Civil War studies now have incorporated guerrilla war and the social history of ordinary people as primary issues to be examined with care. Of course, " major events" like Gettysburg and the Emancipation Proclamation still count, but they are no longer rank ordered as the only truly significant markers of the Civil War as a human experience.

Beyond the centrality of guerrilla warfare as a field central to the study of the Civil War, the political stakes of this debate are considerably greater than they may appear at first. Mark Neely (and Mark Grimsley occasionally) argues that any deviation from the rule of superior American morality as expressed by intrinsically restrained American citizen soldiers was an aberration, that any locale where barbarism broke out was by definition the exception to the rule of restraint. Neely begins his book by telling his readers that he had long been looking for examples that would demonstrate restraint, and that he found them. This methodology, designed to substantiate an abstract theory, strikes me as similar to a lawyer's effort to write a single-minded brief pointing to a unitary preferred outcome. Quite to the contrary, I believe that historians should employ working hypotheses that are always open to revision given the evidence, and should respond to and contain contradictory and complex evidence in their frameworks rather than selecting only those factors that serve to "prove" their pre-existing belief.

This necessity of incorporating inherent ambiguity is especially pertinent when one lives and writes within powerful empires such as the contemporary United States. In such nations, construing the historian's task as building cases for moral exceptionalism (i.e., superiority) while conducting war easily can be harnessed to the task of supporting the building and use of overwhelming military power for purposes of conquest and domination. Civil War historians have a special obligation, I believe, not to twist their work to service contemporary militarism. Rather, they should systematically question the meanings and implications of actual war experiences as opposed to repeating glittering abstractions that can be used to rationalize away highly destructive means while pointing to grand outcomes that may themselves be inconclusive if placed in a wider and more critical context.

If I have learned anything fundamental in my long life as a historian, it is to be wary of the American tendency toward what I have called "perpetually naïve idealism." Living outside the American colossus—if nearby in Canada—for forty years has reinforced my experiences of the tumult of the 1960s, as has some apparently genetic predisposition to disbelieve, and led me to utter skepticism about this faith in American (or any other) national superiority. I also believe that my job, our job, is to stand apart and act as social critics rather than as agents reinforcing mainstream values, a self-distancing grounded in systematic skepticism about all assertions of implicitly unquestioned belief. Perhaps some part of me may remain a disillusioned idealist rather than an utter cynic, but when we write, our goal should be to deal with history as realistically as possible. Of course we assert first principles, even despite ourselves, but we need not accept the belief in glittering abstractions such as nationalistic superiority. Americans are a people among peoples—and a conglomerate rather than a single stock—and the United States is a nation among nations, an empire among empires. National aspiration is inevitably coupled to nationalist blinding to the uses of power. And overreaching leads to tragedy, and often to atrocities, not just down the road, but also in the acts made to construct the road itself.

In my most recent book, *In the Name of God and Country: Reconsidering Terrorism in American History,* I have broadened my critique of the causes and consequences of the belief in American national superiority conjoined to national power by analyzing some of the means by which terrorism has been incorporated as well as combated in the building of the American nation. Unlike many observers, I argue that there is an intrinsic relationship between terrorist acts by nonstate groups and responses by far more powerful governments—both the actions and the reactions constitute terrorism. The rapid advance of governmental power owed a great deal to the overwhelming domination of violent means used by the state, justified by the core nature of American republicanism and Protestant Christianity, both of which contain a core of moral absolutism and self-righteousness that perpetrators engaged in terrorism use to justify their actions. In this book I focused on five key episodes from the period from 1859 to 1902, the epoch when the United States consolidated power at home and first extended itself as an imperial nation abroad: John Brown's raid on Harpers Ferry and the response of the State of Virginia; terrorism during the Civil War, especially race warfare and guerrilla warfare; the organized White Line paramilitary group's destruction of Reconstruction in Mississippi in 1875; the Haymarket Affair and its brutally repressive aftermath; and the Philippine-American War of 1899–1902. "Terrorism," in many forms, is deeply embedded in American history, intrinsic to American habits, self-image, and the institutionalization of force.

I recall that somewhere in his earlier radical phase Eugene Genovese wrote that history comes down to who is riding whom. I agree with that prioritizing of power seeking over every other human activity. Our ideals can be and are often employed to rationalize our greed for domination, for which the employment of implicit and explicit political violence is the easiest and most direct means; this lust for power can be collective as well as individual. If we as historians are powerless to stop the machines of power, we can at least speak truth about them as well as we can muster, and throw sand in the machines.

Rereading this little book several months after writing the first draft, it strikes me that I seem to have suggested that my intellectual life has been far more coherent than was the case. I explored some of the relationships of life experiences linked to my historical work in ways that never had occurred to me before, and those connections do seem to me to have some explanatory power. But in seeking central themes that define my life and work, I both underemphasized my states of confusion and clearly left out other personal and social factors that drove and continue to drive my work and me. There are alternative frameworks that might have been equally or more honest and critical to this project—the ones I chose made sense only of a limited sort. I suppose that such is one limit of all writing.

The clearest instance of omission was a horrifically painful depression when I was forty. Not only was that experience directly related to my choice a few years later to analyze the depression of William T. Sherman in 1861, which almost destroyed him before he rose from the ashes to martial power and then incorporated his depression in his war propaganda, it lent my discussion a certain authenticity. And my melancholy connected me to other people, historical and contemporaneous, in a new way, pushing me to continue to explore the dark side. Other very common and painful experiences such as a divorce and professional setbacks undoubtedly influenced the way I look into history.

However, I must stress that joyful experiences have been at least equally important in shaping my approaches to history and my ability to be a historian. My second marriage, my two sons and their wives, my four grandchildren, friendships, and worthy "enemyships" all have sustained my belief in the power of love. My passion for the theater and for the nonverbal arts, music, visual arts, and most especially modern dance —to which I am wed—and to teaching, reading, and the intense acts of researching and writing have supported me and contributed to my life as a historian. I feel very lucky to have found a deeply satisfying mode of self-expression, one that includes social and political purpose. I also have been sustained and encouraged to soldier on by humor and laughter, many forms of physical and intellectual play, fine food, and dry red wine.

In the spring of 1985, about six months after my bout of depression began to lift with the help of a smart and compassionate psychiatrist and with the support of my enthusiastic students—who did not know of my illness but may have sensed my vulnerability—I had, one night, an extraordinary dream, a psychic lifting. I rarely remember my dreams, but in this instance when I awakened, I remembered every detail.

Two exhausted jazz musicians from a distant culture, ties askew, dust on their shoes, who were both me and other than me in the "logic" or our dreams, walked down into an enormous concrete bunker where some past and lost culture—our culture—was entombed. Tens of thousands of photographs of peoples' faces from this lost society covered the walls all around the room, and at the front of the room sat a battered upright piano, the top of which was covered with manuscript shreds of songs from this unknown place. The piano player fished out one scrap on which was written the opening eight bars of some song left over from back then, sat down, and began to play. Soon the alto sax player joined in. The song was "Yesterdays" by Jerome Kern. As they played, the faces on the walls came alive, and soon the room was filled with their smiles and mutual recognition. Then after about ten minutes, the musicians, exhausted to begin with, began to wind down. But as they did so they realized that the faces were returning to their frozen, dead photographic representations, and so they understood that they just had to keep playing.

Then I woke up.

A couple of weeks later, I shared this dream for the first time with my old friend Dan Horowitz at the annual meeting of the Organization of American Historians. He laughed and said that this was the perfect historian's dream, and he was right. The dream was a part of my mending psyche reminding me of the historian's unique calling—the compelling need to reanimate the experiences of prior cultures, prior peoples. Beyond self-aggrandizement and the necessity of earning a living, that dream expresses what had been and what has remained my vocation, to bear witness to the past as well as I am capable of doing it. Really it is a privilege: I am not certain that any other path would have been a better one.

ACKNOWLEDGMENTS

I THINK I WAS HOOKED on doing history during my freshman year at Oberlin College in the class of Frederic Cheyette, a brilliant and hard-nosed young medievalist who pushed us through tons of reading, topically arranged, and made us argue with him rather than lecturing to us. That took some nerve on our parts, but it was tremendous fun, especially when something I said caused him to argue back heatedly. At Michigan, the late John Higham, in his profound, architectonic lectures in intellectual history, opened the sky while keeping our feet on the ground. And at Northwestern, where I did my doctoral work, Bob Wiebe served as a model teacher when I was one of his teaching assistants, not in the least by requiring that we give lectures to three hundred students, with great feedback that followed. Then and later, he was the most brilliant, toughest, and most supportive reader of my work I have ever had, and his compellingly sweeping and incisive scholarship always encouraged us to take the big and independent view of history. Fellow students Bill Barnes at Oberlin, and Jerry Linderman and Sterling Stuckey at Northwestern, were necessary and welcome companions, as were Dan and Helen Horowitz, then at Harvard and later in California and at Smith College.

At Simon Fraser, where I taught from 1969 to 2008, the late Don Kirschner provided courageous support when the chips were down. I enjoyed the companionship of many colleagues, including Hannah Gay, Martin Kitchen, Dick Debo, the late Doug Cole, Charles Hamilton, Paul Dutton, the late Ron Newton, Robin Fisher, the late Ian Dyck, Andrea Tone, Chris Morris, John Craig, Rod Day, Dick Boyer, Derryl MacLean, Al Seager, Jack Little, and Andrea Geiger. Of course, I have now left out many other people who also contributed to my intellectual development. And many of the hundreds and hundreds of students energized and challenged me in creative ways. Darren Dochuk, Glenn Ryland, Roger Cooter, Rene Hayden, and Mike Egan made particularly strong impacts, as did others.

Many administrators have been supportive over the decades, as have been my agents Bella Pomer and Sydelle Kramer. At Simon Fraser I was blessed with three intelligent deans who knew just how to support independent scholarship: Dale Sullivan, Bob Brown, and John Pierce. Michal Sobel and Mike Zuckerman facilitated a Fulbright year at the University of Haifa in 1980, and Arnon Gutfeld brought me to Tel Aviv University as well. The late Lawrence Stone invited me to the Shelby Cullom Davis Center at Princeton University in 1982–83 and encouraged me plunge ahead on thinking through *Inside War,* without worrying about what "they" might say. The other Davis fellows and many on the Princeton faculty made me feel welcome. The late Martin Ridge and Roy Ritchie made it possible for me to write two books at the Huntington Library, the latter work, *The Making of Robert E. Lee,* with a full year NEH Fellowship. And at the Stanford Humanities Center, Charlie Junkerman and Wanda Corn created a perfect environment for the writing of *Citizen Sherman.* At both these places my fellow fellows were both great fun and incisive critics. Over the years, Stig Forster and Joerg Nagler convened powerful conferences on war and society that furthered my engagement in extranational history. Joerg and Eva Nagler have remained lifelong friends with whom I share work and play.

I have been privileged to co-edit a collection of essays on antislavery with Lew Perry, to co-author a monograph with Anita Clair Fellman, and to write a textbook with Les Gordon and Dan Sutherland. Many readers and editors have shaped my writing and my thinking in major ways, including Bert Wyatt-Brown and Stan Kutler, Malcolm Call, Rachel Toor, Chris Rogers, and Bob Loomis. I have already made clear my debt to Mike Parrish at LSU for this volume, but I would also like to thank Rand Dotson, Alisa Plant, and Neal Novak. Shane White, Leon Litwack, and the late Larry Levine, have been the closest and most inspirational of coworkers. More generally I have valued the friendship of many bookwomen and bookmen with whom I worked or almost worked in many capacities, and the same is true of many conference conveners. Many, many colleagues have been meaningful companions over the years, and I am afraid to name some, as I will forget many others. The same is true of friends all across the world, with whom I have shared a passion for food and wine and travel and fun at least as much as "serious" work. I hope they know who they are.

My family has provided grounding during the ebbs and flows of everyday life in ways that remind me of the sustaining power of love. I would especially like to remember my late parents, David and Sara Fellman, my sister, Laura, my sons, Josh and Eli, and their wives, Mei Ning and Liz, and my darling grandchildren, Sara and Becky, Sam and Isaac. My wife Santa, a compelling dance artist, has supported my work in every way imaginable, including strikingly incisive readings, as we have shared lives of mutuality on every level.

Finally this book is dedicated with immense gratitude to three superb historians—Mike Zuckerman, Chris Phelps, and Bob Wiebe—who helped bring my most controversial and knotty work to light, in discussions with them, in their brilliant readings of drafts of my work, and not least in their interventions with the presses that took the chance to publish what I had to say. I could never measure up to the high standard they set, but they encouraged me to believe what I had to say ought to be heard.